Jung and Catholicism: A Study of Selected Presuppositions Within a Psychological and a Theological System

by Clayton S Meyer

1

Meyer, Clayton Steve

JUNG AND CATHOLICISM: A STUDY OF SELECTED
PRESUPPOSITIONS WITHIN A PSYCHOLOGICAL
AND A THEORETICAL SYSTEM

Drew University
    PH.D.   1980

JUNG AND CATHOLICISM: A STUDY OF

SELECTED PRESUPPOSITIONS WITHIN A

PSYCHOLOGICAL AND A THEOLOGICAL SYSTEM

A Dissertation submitted to the Graduate School

of Drew University in partial fulfillment

of the requirements for the degree

Doctor of Philosophy

Clayton Steve Meyer

Drew University

Madison, New Jersey

1980

Table of Contents

Preface

The basic paradigm of Catholic systematic theology comprises a two-tiered construct of natural and supernatural components. The natural components are felt to flow from the rational abilities of the human person, abilities which in certain ways are capable of touching upon God's existence and some few qualities of His essential being. This natural component of theology supplements the supernatural. Supernatural theology flows from the direct revelation of God and is beyond the discernment of human reason. (1)

The paradigm, from another angle, concerns itself with belief and behavior. Speculative theology concerns itself with determining truth through the pursuit of knowledge. Practical theology concerns itself with the attempt to live a virtuous life.

Schematically, Catholic theology (2) assumes this form:

```
                          (Speculative (Theodicy)
            (Natural       (
            (              (Practical (Ethics)
Theology -------------------------------------------------------------
            (              (Speculative (Systematic Theology)
            (Supernatural (
                          (Practical (Moral Theology)
```

Natural theology is a clear and a substantial part of the Catholic mosaic. It presents, as it were, an opening statement in the dialogue with an empirical psychology bent on assessing human structure and human fulfillment.(3) For a psychologist like Jung, the fulcrum between religion and psychology is natural theology. As we shall see later, his view toward supernatural theology is ambivalent.

At times it appears that the whole supernatural portion of the paradigm could simply be discounted as having no value to our study. However, this is not the case. Jung felt that every theological manifestation, natural and supernatural, has its psychological correlate (4). Everything theological can be translated into something psychological. Every supernatural occurrence thus is subject to psychological commentary.

But it is not only Jung who disregards the paradigmatic divisions. While Catholicism maintains a strict separation of the speculative branches of the two theologies, it has serious problems in doing so in the practical theologies, particularly in regard to Moral Theology (5). What should be a fairly solidified and absolute aspect of the schema (vis-a-vis Systematic theology) is, in fact, in a precarious position.

Factually, Moral theology accepts and amplifies many of the arguments addressed in the natural science of ethics. For more than fifteen hundred years the Church did not even consider Moral theology as a separate discipline. Historically, it is rooted in the Council of Trent and its desire to train good confessors (6). As this study unfolds, it will be clear that the structure and fulfillment of the human person are subject to considerable stress if viewed in the traditional Catholic moral terms (7). The Second Vatican Council hints diplomatically at the problem in these words: "The human race has passed from a rather static concept of reality to a more dynamic evolutionary one (8)."

Is it possible, in view of the mutual crossing-over of natural and supernatural theology by both parties, to maintain any semblance of methodological integrity? The answer seems to be yes as long as we do not mislead ourselves as to the actual or potential weaving together of the natural and supernatural components. Ultimately our concern remains the inter-structural compatibility of two sets of presuppositions each of which claim to lead to valid interpretations of human existence.

From its beginning the Church was confronted with the problem of contrary and contradictory interpretations of reality. In its process of self-reflection and self-understanding, the Church absorbed certain explanations of reality while discarding and repudiating others. This process gradually evolved into a cohesive and comprehensive substructure (9) integral to an understanding of Catholicism. This substructure, or synthetic net, constitutes the underpinnings of Catholic systematic theology. For Catholics, theology is the science of the Christian faith. As Karl Rahner explains it,

> Theology is, among other things, an ecclesiastical science of faith. Human inter-subjectivity is at its peak in faith. Since faith, the hearing of the revelation directed to the people of God, is the faith of the Church and faith within the Church, theology is necessarily ecclesiastical. Otherwise it ceases to be itself and become the prey of the wayward subjective spirituality of the individual, which is today less fitted than ever to be the cohesive force of a community. Since the faith of the Church is necessarily linked tot he historical word of divine revelation, Church theology is necessarily dependent on Scripture and tradition. Since the Church, as the community of faith, is an institutional society, Church theology is essentially related to the Magisterium in the Church (10).

Elsewhere, Rahner explains the problem which is making "Catholic theology" more difficult to discern. He states,

> There have always been 'schools' of theology upholding contradictory opinions, starting from different assumptions and developing different patterns of thought. A pluralism of this type in theology is not new and it has always been a principle in the Church that it should be either tolerated or expressly approved of. But theologies today are displaying

8

a pluralism of a different type, one that cannot be now reduced to unity. There will be more and more theologies, which will not be able to follow each other adequately, though this of course does not mean that they will be simply juxtaposed without influencing each other. On the contrary, a new type of effort at mutual tolerance, mutual influence and mutual criticism will be necessary, much more than hitherto. The Magisterium, nourished too exclusively by a certain type of Roman theology, will have to find new ways of controlling and fostering this pluralism (11).

Though our age is clearly a turning point in the appreciation of pluralistic theologies, that has not yet become a reality for Catholic theology insofar as it relates to the Magisterium. In the discussion presented here, the focus will be on the magisterially conscious theology, though an awareness of what configurations such theology might take in the future is beyond our imagining. It is certain that in whatever direction Catholic theology moves, it will still be appreciably influenced by the Magisterium.

The magisterial theology that historically parallels Jungian psychology falls basically within Thomistic parameters. It would be erroneous to equate that specific theological articulation with the generic threads of Catholic theology that are represented by other schools. On the other hand, it would be misleading to say that the Thomistic school was simply one among many; in actuality, it found a 'most favored status' in the institutional Church and its premises underlay the manual theology so prominent until the II Vatican Council.

The Magisterium, in the context of this dissertation, refers to the teaching function of the Catholic Church. Ordinarily this function is lodged in the Councils and in the Popes, and the degree of their authority is disputed, except in those formal articulations of Catholic belief that are infrequently pronounced in a solemn fashion. The Catholic theologians who reacted to Jung and who are here considered constructed their perceptions in the light of what they thought the magisterial teaching to be in their time. We must always keep in mind that during much of the time Jung was writing, the Magisterium was absorbed with the modernist controversy. This weaving together of Magisterium and theologian in an historical setting accounts for the consensual reaction that emerged in assessing Jung's writings.

An example of magisterically determined doctrine involves the concept of the soul. It was not until Vatican II that the Magisterium broke out of the body-soul schema and came into line with the approach of the modern era. The key word is now person and not soul (12). Both the Catholic and Jungian perspective on the structure and fulfillment of the human person. It will indicate in a substantive way the actual complementarity of two systems that purport to explain human existence and interpret human activity.

In this investigation, "system" refers to a comprehensive paradigm which accounts for meaningful human experience. The ideal paradigm is so constructed that it retains a basic continuity of explanation and no significant element of that explanation contradicts any other element.

The viability of this investigation rests upon the fact that the areas under examination are essential components of both systems. This is neither to suggest that the vocabulary or setting is a constant for both systems, nor is it to imply that there is a simple process by which elements in one system can be interchanged with that of another. But precisely because they are systems, each has taken a position on questions which men and women pose as they seek to understand themselves and their behavior (13).

Each question, then, has its counterpart in the other system. Some correlations are obvious, some are disguised. Others are contrary or contradictory.

Jung was a system-builder (14). Though his psychology has a common association with analysis, it has, in reality, all the dimensions of a synthesis. Jung is clearly in the classical tradition. He did not deal with reality on an issue-by-issue basis alone, but instead he tried to create a framework in which the experience of the thousands of people with whom he worked took on meaning.

Upon reflection, it is not unusual that the Catholic theological aggregate be labeled a system, too. Contemporary theology reserves the term "dogmatics" to material revealed by God, and designates as "systematics" the general theological schema. In Catholic theology, 'systematics' has a two-fold meaning: (1) the process of an orderly and schematized study of believes, and (2) the awareness that these beliefs do indeed constitute an interlocking system.

Since Jung has chosen in his system to relate to religious experience at nearly every level, we are dealing with two relatively correlative systems. In each system critical decisions are made at the elementary stage. These decisions determine the inevitable outcome of each system.

Summarily, this is an investigation of the correlation and compatibility of three of the fundamental presuppositions which underlie the Catholic and the Jungian systems. There will be five chapters to this study. The initial chapter will deal with placing the entire discussion in its appropriate environment. Each of the three succeeding chapters will be devoted to a presupposition. There is the actual determination of what each system maintains as its presuppositions. This is followed by observations that each system makes about the other's perspective. The final chapter will draw together the study and channel it to the focal point of human structure and self-realization. It suggests how the Catholic tradition can, through utilizing the Jungian system, better understand its own mythology and facilitate what Jung calls 'modern man's search for his soul.'

As time passes, fewer human disciplines, theology included, make the audacious claim that any single perspective is able by itself to exhaust the configurations of human experience. Yet the imperial attitude persists. Among others, some theologians and some psychologists claim that their science most adequately explains human existence. There is academic pushing and shoving to mark off territory for one's own discipline. The situation is reminiscent of the race for the New World. It is into this kind of atmosphere that we introduce Carl Gustav Jung and his analytical psychology (15).

Depth psychology, in part, came into being when religion began to fail its adherent's needs (16). There are those who maintain that classical psychology must seek two objectives if it wants to contribute fully to the development of the human person; 1) discontinue being the shadow-side of religious expression, and 2) avoid being a moral surrogate for religious imperatives.

Jung considers the spiritual meanings of the person to be the legitimate concern of psychology. Indeed, if there is a close relationship between theology and psychology, Jung has been in the forefront of those who have sought it. It is to his work that we must turn if we wish to come closer to discovering whether there can be a valid re-mythologization of religious experience, and whether there is indeed a legitimate link between psychology and theology.

Chapter I

"A small mistake in the beginning is a big one in the end"

St. Thomas quoting Averroes <u>De Ente et Essentia</u>, I.

THE PSYCHOLOGICAL AND THEOLOGICAL PRELUDE

<u>The Jungian View</u>

We can gain some insight into Jung's position by observing that not a single Catholic who has written extensively on Jung has been able to accept Jung's presuppositions without serious reservations (17). The common complaint seems to eventually drift to Jung's infatuation with Kantianism and to an intimation that Jung is both a psychological and theological modernist. And if Jung were Catholic, that would put him at odds with the Magisterium.

"Modernism" is a generic term given to the proposals of a multi-national group of European theologians whose purpose was to "modernize" the Church. To counter this movement, Pope Pius X in 1907 issued a list of sixty-five items deemed untenable for Catholic belief. Pius shored-up the values of rational knowledge by deprecating any agnosticism issuing from any combination of subjectivism, phenomenalism, and relativism. He further denounced the idea of immanentism, according to which human consciousness bears in itself, virtually, every truth, even divine, which is developed under the stimulus of the religious sense.

There is no doubt that Jung was sympathetic to these modernistic positions and developed his psychology upon some of their postulates. Two of the more prominent consequences are; 1) the impossibility of demonstrating the existence of a personal God, and 2) religion (18) and revelation are natural products of the unconscious, dogma being its provisional expression, subject to continual evolution. We can see Jung's bond to modernism if we look at Ernesto Buonaiuti, a staunch defender of modernism in Italy, and at the same time a devout disciple of Jung (19).

In analyzing modernism, we must credit Jung with the sterling observations he made about a different kind of "modernism" in his Modern Man in Search of a Soul. In that work Jung describes the modernist as one who is fully conscious of the present. He maintains that the crux of the spiritual problem of today is to be found in the fascination which psychic life exerts upon modern man (20). Jung says that the various forms of religion no longer appear to the modern man to come from within - to be expressions of his own psychic life; for him they are to be classed with the things of the outer world. There is a magisterial affinity that easily coincides with Jungian views such as these. However, when the Jungian argument unfolds, that affinity quickly lapses into disagreement.

16

The theme of <u>Modern Man in Search of a Soul</u> is not the focus of this work. Though it has definite repercussions for religion, such as a topic would lead into a study of whether psychology is religion's replacement (21). Though that possibility touches upon our subject matter, it is a secondary question and will not be extensively considered.

We can gain further insight into Jung's position by observing that there is a wide and controversial range of opinions about his psychological contribution. These opinions are from colleagues, not theologians. Authors compile lavish lists of Jungian credits, claiming Jung has discovered everything from the inadequacies of Freud to the fact that religious meaning is the basic function of the human psyche.

The exuberance must be tempered. A random survey of general psychology books will usually show a dozen or more pages devoted to Freud's contributions to psychology while Jung may get a page or two (22). A sampling of psychological observations about Jung shows the following: "For most of us scientifically trained occidentals who worship objectivity and stress causality. . . this basically oriental approach to reality. . . stresses the <u>configuration</u> rather than the <u>sequence</u> of events (23). Despite strenuous effort at understanding, much of Jung's writings simply do not 'make sense' to us." The French psychoanalyst, Maryse Choisy (24), writes that, "Latin minds, fond of rigor and clarity, objective to the obscure side of Jung, his very religiosity. With Jung we lose on both counts. The Jungian demonstration becomes a begging of the principle in question. Personally, I admire Jung very much, but for the work that I have to undertake, I need an indisputably scientific base (25).

Jung constantly reminds us that he was brought to a consideration of religious problems through the experiences of his patients. In fact, for Jung, psychology and psychotherapy were spawned by crises that eventually came to face the religious personality in the west (26). Many were unable to identify with traditional Christianity. Separated from its symbolism and its language, alienated Christians were driven to an awareness of certain psychic components in the personality whose significance was not previously considered. Those psychic components constitute the unconscious. An evolving and troubled Christianity prompted the need to search for a self-knowledge to fill a critical vacuum. The scientific form of that self-knowledge we know by the name of psychology (27).

Jung states that the psychological interest of the present time is an indication that modern man expects something from the psyche which the outer world has not given him: doubtless something which our religion ought to contain, but no longer does contain, at least for modern man (28). For him the various forms of religion no longer appear to come from within, from the psyche; they seem more like items from the inventory of the outside world (29).

Jung feels that the crux of the spiritual problem today is to be found in the fascination which the psyche holds for modern man. If we are pessimists, we shall call it a sign of decadence; if we are optimistically inclined, we shall see in it the promise of a far-reaching spiritual change in the Western world. At all events, it is a significant phenomenon. It touches those irrational and --- as history shows --- incalculable psychic forces which transform the life of people and civilizations in ways that are unforeseen and unforeseeable (30). These are the forces, still invisible to many persons today, which are at the bottom of the present "psychological" interest. The fascination of the psyche is not by any means a morbid perversity. It is an attraction so strong that it does not shrink even from what it finds repellent (31).

Jung embarked upon a venture to explain the unconscious in terms of its structure and its process. Since the unconscious is by its very definition beyond our consciousness, Jung was compelled to rely upon a repertoire of hypothetical components to explain its structure (32). He relied upon assumptions drawn from certain types of conscious experience to guide him. And he relied on terms already in use, though he shared their meanings and was attacked for his linguistic ambiguity.

About the terminology problem, Jung says that we can readily agree that physiological characteristics are something that can be seen, touched, measured. But in psychology not even the meanings of words are fixed. "The state of our knowledge might be compared with natural philosophy in the Middle Ages. . .that is to say, everybody in psychology knows better than everybody else (33). There are only opinions about unknown facts. Hence the psychologist has an almost invincible tendency to cling to the security of things that appear to be known and defined.

As science is dependent on the definiteness of verbal concepts, it is incumbent upon the psychologist to make conceptual distinctions and to attach definite names to certain groups of psychic facts, regardless of whether somebody else has a different conception of the meaning of this term or not. The only thing he has to consider is whether the name he uses agrees, in its ordinary usage, with the psychic facts designated by it (34).

At the same time, Jung maintains, "The psychologist must rid himself of the common notion that the name explains the psychic fact it denotes. The name should mean to him no more than a mere cipher, and his whole conceptual system should be to him no more than a trigonometrical survey of a certain geographical area, in which the fixed points of reference are indispensable in practice but irrelevant in theory (35).

Theoretically, according to Jung, no limits can be set to the field of consciousness, since it is capable of indefinite extension (36). Empirically, however, it always finds its limit when it comes up against the unknown. This consists of everything we do not know, which, therefore, is not related to the ego as the center of the field of consciousness (37). The unknown falls into two groups of objects; those which are outside and can be experienced by the senses, and those which are inside and are experienced immediately. The first group comprises the unknown in the outer world; the second the unknown in the inner world. We call this latter territory the unconscious (38).

The somatic basis of the ego consists, then, of conscious and unconscious factors. The same is true of the psychic basis; on the one hand the ego rests on the total field of consciousness, and on the other, on the sum total of unconscious contents. These fall into three groups: first, temporarily subliminal contents that can be reproduced voluntarily (memory); second, unconscious contents that cannot be reproduced voluntarily; third, contents that are not capable of becoming conscious at all. Group two can be inferred from the spontaneous eruption of subliminal contents into consciousness. Group three is hypothetical; it is a logical inference from the facts underlying group two. It contains contents which have not erupted into consciousness or which never will.

The personality as a total phenomenon does not coincide with the ego; that is, with the conscious personality but forms an entity that has to be distinguished from the ego. Jung has suggested that we call the total personality the self. Though present, the self cannot be fully known. The ego not only can do nothing against the self, but is sometimes actually assimilated by unconscious components of the personality that are in the process of development and is greatly altered by them (39).

We have seen that, from the standpoint of the psychology of consciousness, the unconscious can be divided into three groups of contents. But from the standpoint of the psychology of the personality a two-fold division ensues: an "extra-conscious" psyche whose contents are personal, and an "extra-conscious" psyche whose contents are impersonal and collective. The first group comprises contents which are integral components of the individual personality and could therefore just as well be conscious; the second group forms, as it were, an omnipresent, unchanging, and everywhere identical quality or substrate of the psyche per se.

All of this is, of course, no more than an hypothesis. But we are driven to it by the peculiar nature of the empirical material, not to mention the high probability that the general similarity of psychic processes in all individuals must be based on an equally general and impersonal principle that conforms to law, just as the instinct manifesting itself in the individual is only the partial manifestation of an instinctual substrate common to all.

Many of the processes and complexities of the Jungian unconscious are of only indirect concern to this study. Some particular aspects, however, do not belong to any discussion of self realization and they will appear later. Since we are here portraying the Jungian unconscious in broad out-line, mention should be made of Jung's archetype.

Archetypes are typical, universal, uniform, and regular modes of apprehension which manifest themselves everywhere in identical fashion, not as concrete forms but as forms without content, representing merely the possibilities of a certain type of perception and action. Jung depicts archetypes as psychic forms which, like the instincts, are common to all men and women (40). The total personality can be affected by them through a process of identification.

The archetype of the self is the most important element composing the unconscious. It is the goal of the psychotherapeutic process. Moreno describes the archetype of the self as an expression of human wholeness, of the totality of man; that is to say, of both his conscious and unconscious contents (41). To achieve wholeness in man, as in the deity, the opposites are drawn into a paradoxical unity; good and evil, conscious and unconscious, masculine and feminine, dark and light, are raised to a synthesis symbolically expressed by the conjuctio oppositorum.

Because of its importance and centrality to Jungian thought, the idea of the archetype has been subject to criticism. A student of Jung, Victor White (42), writes "Matters are complicated by the fact that, in his efforts to make himself understood. Jung frequently describes archetypes in terms borrowed from other disciplines --- biology, optics, nuclear physics, crystallography --- and by correlating them with philosophical concepts taken from Plato, Kant and Schopenhaur (43)." Phenomena, postulates, hypothesis, theories, models, analogies, and metaphors are not always too clearly distinguished from one another, and the very quantity and variety of descriptions are not at all easy to correlate, and may suggest a certain vagueness and lack of precision to all but the most patient and leisured reader.

Raymond Hostie writes that Jung did in fact endeavor to discover a physiological substrate with which he could connect the archetypes, hoping in this way to avoid the accusation of inventing "mystical" things (44). Not that he went in for any anatomical line of argument and an unverifiable historical assertion. The archetypes are not innate because they are acquired, but not individual, because they are acquired by men and women as a whole (45).

Pressed by his critics, Jung reached for a physical explanation to support his archetypal hypothesis. The explanation, biologically untenable, is that the brain, having had to try at every moment to solve the same problems, has taken certain "creases." These creases, or tracks of ideas, have become encrusted in the brain and now direct our conscious activity. As soon as consciousness relaxes, the unconscious takes up its normal course again and reacts as it has been reacting for century after century (46).

Jung's attempts to bind the psychological to the physical were indicative of his earlier studies. In fact his work on the galvanometer and his research on the observed behavior of extraverts and introverts constitute, for behavioral psychologists especially, the only credible contribution Jung has made to psychology. However, Jung did not see things that way.

If we trace the evolution of Jung's thought we see that between 1915 and 1935 his writings focused almost exclusively on analytical psychology. During this period Jung was involved with the more conventional concerns of psychology. In the early 1930's we can detect a shift. Jung suggests that gnosticism and medieval alchemy play a role in understanding the unfolding of the unconscious and the development of the therapeutic process. And from 1935 until his death in 1961, Jung made some of the central dogmas of Catholicism the object of his psychological studies. As the one-time heir apparent to Freud, as a Swiss Protestant, and as a scholar who insisted on his unflagging devotion to science and the empirical method, how did Jung find his way into the religious concerns that came to absorb so much of his time (47)?

Jung is not a theologian. He tells us, "Since I am not chiefly concerned with theology but rather with the layman's picture of theological concepts (a fact you must constantly bear in mind), I am liable to make many apparent contradictions. I am thinking --- as a psychologist --- about all sorts of erroneous notions which do exist in spite of higher criticism and accurate exegesis and all the achievements of theological research (48).

He goes on to say in The Symbolic Life that:

> My object is the general condition of the Christian mind, and not theology, where I am wholly incompetent. . . I am concerned with dogmas, prejudices, illusions, and errors and every kind of doubt in the layman's mind, and I try to get a certain order into that chaos by the means accessible to a layman, i.e., to myself as a representative of the humble 'ignoramus.' (49).

> Instead of using the term God you say 'unconscious,' instead of Christ 'self,' instead of incarnation 'integration of the unconscious,' instead of salvation or redemption 'individuation,' instead of crucifixion or sacrifice on the Cross 'realization of the four functions or of wholeness.' I think it is no disadvantage to religious tradition if we can see how far it coincides with psychological experiences (50). On the contrary, it seems to be a most welcome aid of understanding religious traditions (51).

Jung is very direct in his questioning of religion's significance: "The world --- so far as it has not completely turned its back on tradition --- has long stopped wanting to hear a "message;" it would rather be told what the message means. The words that resound from the pulpit are incomprehensible and cry for an explanation (52)."

Jung asks how has the death of Christ brought us redemption when no one feels redeemed? In what way is Jesus a God-Man and what is such a being? What is the Trinity about, and the parthenogenesis, the eating of the body and the drinking of the blood, and all the rest of it? What connection can there be between the world of such concepts and the everyday world, whose material reality is the concern of natural science on the widest possible scale (53).

At least sixteen hours out of twenty-four we live exclusively in this everyday world, and the remaining eight we spend preferably in an unconscious condition. When and where does anything take place to remind us even remotely of phenomena like angels, miraculous feedings, beatitudes, the resurrection of the dead, etc.? It was therefore something of a discovery to find that during the unconscious state of sleep intervals occur, called "dreams," which occasionally contain scenes having a not inconsiderable resemblance to the motifs of mythology (54). For the myths are miracle tales and treat of all those things which, very often are also objects of belief (55).

Even intelligent people, according to Jung, no longer understand the value and purpose of symbolical truth, and the spokesmen of religion have failed to deliver an apologetic suited to the spirit of the age (56). Insistence on the bare concretism of dogma, or ethics for ethics' sake, or even a humanization of the Christ-figure coupled with inadequate attempts to write his biography, are singularly unimpressive. Symbolical truth is exposed undefended to the attacks of scientific thought, which can never do justice to such a subject, and in the face of this competition has been unable to hold its ground (57). The truth, however, still remains to be proved. Exclusive appeals to faith are a hopeless petitio principii, for it is the manifest improbability of symbolical truth that prevents people from believing it (58).

Instead of insisting so glibly on the necessity of faith, the theologians, according to Jung, should see what can be done to make this faith possible. But that means placing symbolical truth on a new foundation --- a foundation which appeals not only to sentiment, but to reason. And this can only be achieved by reflecting how it came about in the first place that humanity needed the improbability of religious statements, and what it signifies when a totally different spiritual reality is superimposed on the sensuous and tangible actuality of this world.

Jung maintains that the more highly developed men of our time do not want to be guided by a creed or dogma; they want to understand (59). So it is not surprising if they throw aside everything they do not understand; and religious symbols, being the least intelligible of all, are generally the first to go overboard. The sacrifice of the intellect demanded by a positive belief is a violation against which the conscience of the more highly developed individual rebels.

According to Jung, the medical psychotherapist must make clear to his more educated patients the foundations of religious experience, and set them on the road to where such an experience becomes possible. "If therefore, as a doctor and scientist, I analyze abstruse religious symbols and trace them back to their origins, my sole purpose is to conserve, through understanding, the values they represent, and to enable people to think symbolically once more, as the early thinkers of the Church were still able to do (60)."

Jung answers us that this is far from implying an arid dogmatism. It is only when we, today, think dogmatically, that our thought becomes antiquated and no longer accessible to modern man. Hence, a way has to be found which will again make it possible for him to participate spiritually in the substance of the Christian message (61).

To this point, there are four summary items that merit attention. First, Jung's "modernism" tendencies create serious problems for establishing some kind of rapprochement with magisterial thinking. Second, the fluidity of Jungian vocabulary allows terms to lose their previous definitiveness and exclusivity. Third, Jung's constructs for explaining the unconscious are extraordinarily creative though necessarily abstract. Finally, though Jung spent more than twenty-five years correlating his psychological constructs with Catholic dogmas, he did so not on the basis of his theological background and study, but rather on the premise that religious symbolism and behavior are a mirror of unconscious psychic structure and dynamics.

The Catholic View

We need to turn now to the other partner in this study. What does Catholicism and its proponents say to Jung? How do they respond to the observations he has so far made? We begin by noting what Jung says about some of the criticism he has received.

> I have never refused the bitter-sweet drink of philosophical criticism, but have taken it with caution, a little at a time. All too little my opponents will say; almost too much, my own feeling tells me. All too easily does self-criticism poison one's naivete, that priceless possession, or rather gift, which no creative person can do without.
>
> At any rate, philosophical criticism has helped me to see that every psychology --- my own included --- has the character of a subjective confession. And yet I must

prevent my critical powers from destroying my creativeness. I know well enough that every word I utter carries with it something of myself --- of my special and unique self with its particular history and its own particular world. Even when I deal with empirical date I am necessarily speaking about myself. But it is only by accepting this as inevitable that I can serve the cause of man's knowledge of man. Knowledge rests not upon truth alone, but upon error also (62).

As one might suspect, there are a number of theological opinions about Jung (63). Apart from a consensus that his work has implications for theology, good or bad, there is no clear agreement about its value. And in some instances there are strikingly contradictory assessments of his work.

According to Moreno, Jung's discoveries in psychology are of great implication in theology because these discovers, which the theologian is ready to welcome, prove that religion is man's most important instinct (64). They also prove that the symbols, dogmas, and images of Christianity are archetypal and --- save the exception of the quaternity --- in perfect agreement with the needs of our unconscious. According to this author, there lies Jung's greatest contribution to theology. Christianity fits perfectly the psychological needs of man, even the needs unknown to us because they are unconscious. As Moreno assess him, Jung has revealed the primary importance of paradigms, or archetypes, as against the motley variety of the contingency of daily experience. There exist natural tendencies in man to escape from the particular and contingent in order to attain the universal, the permanent, the absolute (65). Even the intuitive experience of the primitive concerning myth, although existential and spontaneous, is chiefly paradigmatical and exemplar. In this sense Jung is not an existential philosopher; for him, the essence is more important than the concrete existence and the general patterns bear more weight in life than the concrete situation in which they appear (66).

For Eugene Merlin, Jung is important for theology because he sees the intimate connection between the spiritual and psychic life of a person. For him, growth in one is necessary for growth and health in the other. Indeed, the spiritual and psychic life basically are one; their fortunes are to a great extent indistinguishable (67).

Merlin ties in Jung's work with Chardin's The Divine Mileiu (68). The Christian mandate to build the earth includes building the human person, the high point of the earth. This does not mean just a conquering of our surroundings and a growth in factual and speculative knowledge, but also an exploring and advancing of our psyche. Thus, if we as Christians are to be passionate about the earth, we must be passionate about our depths. If nothing is profane and everything is in the process of divinization, then those who profess religion must also concern themselves with the internal world of men and women.

Michael Fordham maintains that the contribution of analytical psychology to religion consists in bringing religious experience home to the individual in a way which nothing else can do; it brings it home as a psychological fact (69). This is surely a most important event. Moreover, in bringing home the possibility of becoming a whole or real individual we are following, in however humbl and insignificant a way, what religion has always termed the will of God.

William Johnson represents a chorus of theologians who claim that Jung's psychology is nothing more than a disguised mysticism. Johnson states that the basic theological problem in Jung's analytic psychology is its implicit mysticism, and we are permitted to speak of theological problems in Jung's psychology because Jung himself speaks of his psychology as a redemptive spiritual gestalt (70).

For this school of critics, depth psychologies must of necessity deal with abstractions, paradoxes, linguistic impression, and scientifically unverifiable hypotheses. The reason for this is simply that the discipline is involved structurally in an area of experience which is non-cognitive and spiritual. The mystic's language and experience perhaps best suit the needs of the psychologist as he attempts to explain what he is about.

Jung wants to avoid metaphysical constructs because they impose experience that he discovers (71). He can speak of the "transcendence of problems," which for him means that a problem cannot be resolved, but can only be experienced, and experienced in such a way as to provide the content for a systematic analysis. And Jung must also dodge the logical construct because his realm of experience is one not congruent with neat intellectual order; he takes his experiences where he finds them.

Problems for the theology emerge once Jung establishes that the wholeness of personality rises from within the individual psyche itself. As soon as this thesis is affirmed, it immediately detracts from the theological claims of the Jewish and Christian faiths. What both Judaism and Christianity affirms is the historic objectivity of biblical events, events which constitute for the believer the source of his salvation; that is, of man's total spiritual and psychic wholeness. What Jung appears to have done is to reduce the historical fact of the biblical events to an extension and deepening of the consciousness (72).

Though not a Christian, perhaps the most sever of Jung's critics is Martin Buber (73). It is Buber's thesis that faith is not a feeling in the soul of man but an entrance into reality, an entrance in the whole reality without reduction and curtailment. The religious essence in every religion can be found in its highest certainty. That is the certainty that the meaning of existence is open and accessible in the actual lived concrete, not above the struggle with reality but in it.

According to Buber, Jung's definition of religion is a relation to psychic events pure and simple. This cannot mean anything other than a relation to one's own soul; it is implied by this that it is not a relation to a being or reality which, no matter how fully it may from time to time descend to the human soul, always remain transcendent to it (74). More precisely, it is not the relation of an I to a Thou. This I/Thou relation is, however, the way in which the unmistakably religious of all ages have understood their religion even if they longed most intensely to let their I be mystically absorbed into that Thou (75).

According to J. McLeish, Jung himself has said that his writings are not really intended for believers; his ideal reader would seem to be a cultured and intelligent scientist or professional man who, as a result of his training, never thinks about religion or imagines that it could have any relevance for him (76). McLeish contends that, in a sense, Jung's writings are too difficult for a person with a theological background; such a reader has too many prejudices and preconceptions.

The Marxian parallel suggests itself. Just as Marx thought the real study of political science, religion, and all human disciplines was economics, so Jung believes it is psychology. Therefore a theologian who studies theology for its own sake misses the point. Jung suggest that theologians may have lost the capacity for understanding that objective truth is not enough for human beings.

Unless the truths of religion are psychologically true and can be experienced by the individual they are lifeless and must lack the essential truth of religion insofar as such truths require an experiential basis. Jung does not so much say these things as illustrate them again and again diverse contexts which invariably have a human reference. In the relations between God and the human person, Jung is concerned with the human aspect and hardly at all concerned with God as He is in Himself.

The technical meaning that Jung gives the word "God adds to the difficulty and confusion of his religious readers. Jung's "God" includes any abstract person or thing that has been designated as divine. Jung does not even mean the ontological reality of this God of his, but only its repercussions in the human psyche.

Reading Jung, the Christian has a constant sensation of deja vue. But everything is tilted just enough to cause an uncomfortable frustration. Whether Jung is talking about God, analyzing dogma, or explaining religion, something inadequate or inordinate crops up in every area.

Moreno points out the problem when he says that Otto's (77) and Jung's approach to religion stresses too much the primitive and archaic conception of religious man, and fear rather than love. In that kind of mysticism fear is an essentially a manifestation of religious experience as is love. If God is duality, fear has to be a factor as important as love. In consequence, Jung chooses Nicholaus of Claus, Meister Eckhart, and especially Jacob Bohme as a authentic exemplars of Christian mysticism, ignoring Teresa of Jesus and John of the Cross. As Otto puts it, "In our Western mysticism the writer in whom the non-rationally 'dreadful' and 'demonic' phase of the numinous remains a most living element is Jacob Bohme (78)."

This spectral range of theological assessment of Jung would run in this fashion: extremely helpful --- harmless --- harmful --- extremely dangerous. Generally, those who are situated in the extremely dangerous zone see the Jungian enterprise as an attempt to reduce the whole of religion to psychology. That reduction is accomplished, in their minds, through a series of observations and conclusions that are unjustified, unverifiable, and often untrue.

R.B. Nordberg states that one must object, as usual, to what Jung says about psychology and what he does with it. Nordberg contends that throughout his career, Jung periodically insisted that he was a militant empiricist, whereas he was obviously metaphysical to the core. In <u>Mysterium Conjunctionis,</u> he announces that "psychology cannot advance any argument either for or against the objective validity of any metaphysical view," then uses this "psychology" to reach such conclusions as that "the mystical experiences of the saints are no different from other effects of the unconscious (79)."

In his review of <u>Mysterium Conjunctionis</u>, Nordberg maintains that Jung's metaphysic is one of naturalistic reductionism, a psychologism which takes a tour of Christian theology and reduces it all to tricks of the unconscious. Yet Jung never seems quite sure. He wrote feelingly of a young man who "has only the mystery of his living soul to set against the overwhelming might and brutality of collective convictions." Perhaps he knew an old man with the same problem (80).

Carl Alfred Meier observes that if a cure, at least in the field of neurosis, depends upon the recognition of the religious function of the soul, then the conclusion may be drawn that it is remoteness from God which is the cause for the effect termed "neurosis (81)." The reintroduction of the religious function would then serve as a therapeutic function. In other words, what many of Jung's patients "lacked" was exactly this religious function and its conscious recognition. This explanation, according to Meier, can be called a logically and philosophically inadmissible simplification or generalization (82). The real situation is usually much more complicated (83).

It is unfortunate that Jung makes little distinction between metaphysics, theology and faith. These three different fields are lumped under the same single heading, "the religious point of view." Because of this Jungian assimilative perception, two reactions regularly occur. First, there is a general trend to widen the Kantian area of what is "unknown," and there is, secondly, the counter-reaction by disciplines with the supposedly "unknown" material to demonstrate that Jung is neither knowledgeable nor sophisticated about non-psychological matters. As an example of the problem, let us look at "reality."

Jung says that people always speak of man and his psychology as though there were "nothing but" that psychology. In the same way one always talks of "reality" as though it were the only one. Jung maintains that reality is simply what works in a human soul and not what is assumed by certain people to work there, and about which prejudiced generalizations are wont to be made (84).

> Elsewhere Jung writes,

> For the purposes of psychology, I think it best to abandon the notion that we are today in anything like a position to make statements about the nature of the psyche that are 'true' or 'correct.' The best that we can achieve is true expression. By true expression, I mean an open avowal and detailed presentation of everything that is subjectively observed.

Jung maintains that whatever appears in the psyche is psychologically "true" (85).

The most profuse of Catholic commentators on Jung, Victor White, takes serious exception to Jung's view on what is "real" and "true." He says to call any idea "psychologically true" simply on the ground that is exists is at least open to misunderstanding, and we are left guessing what could possibly be "psychologically false" (86).

Moreover, White says, it is at least unusual to call a "truth" that which is merely "a fact and not a judgment." It has been generally agreed for some millennia that a bare fact or the simple observation of a fact is neither true nor false, and that truth or falsehood can be expressed only in a judgment. The natural sciences have not departed from this usage. They have become very hesitant to claim the words "true" or "false" at all, but would anyway not claim them except for judgments embodied in statements or equations.

White argues that while the empirical psychologist can check his patient's mother-complex against the "real" (ie., complex-free and empirically knowable and verifiable) mother, there is no "real God" in any way knowable and verifiable to which the God-complex can be compared. To the psychologist as such, there is no God independent of the complex. Indeed such preconceptions should logically force him to the conclusion that this complex cannot be other than a purely irrational fact; he has no means of ascertaining whether it is a complex about anything. It just is. There are no rational statements about God, no products of directed thinking with which it can be compared. Thus, the very possibility that religion could develop into an adult, rational, voluntary relationship --- such as he may hope and expect of his patient's relationship to his parents when the complex has been analyzed --- is a priori excluded. Jung, to illustrate the confusion of the interdisciplinary problems, says,

> I can hardly draw a veil over the fact that we psychotherapists ought really to be philosophers or philosophic doctors --- or rather that we already are so, though we are unwilling to admit it because of the glaring contrast between our work and what passes for philosophy in the universities. We could also call it religion in statu nascendi, for in the vast confusion that reigns at the roots of life there is no line of division between philosophy and religion. Nor does the unrelieved strain of the psychotherapeutic situation, with its host of impressions and emotional disturbances, leave us much leisure for the systematization of thought. Thus we have no clear exposition of guiding principles drawn from life to offer either to the philosophers or to the theologians (87).

Igor Caruso responds by saying, "We do not conform to the strict condition laid down by Jung, that psychology must remain within its own proper sphere, without exceeding it 'by such things as metaphysical assertions or other confessions of faith'" (88). He suggests that it is, of course, meritorious if a scientific investigator confines his method to the strictest empiricism; but after giving solemn assurance of this methodological limitation, he is not entitled to propound "metaphysical assertions" in a round-about way, under an empiricist cover.

Caruso argues that nobody may stop the scientist from arranging his empirically acquired data into an orderly and significant whole by means of a logical process, and this applies even more to the psychologist. This is precisely why even those psychologists who, frightened as they were of "philosophizing" as of an embarrassing disease, could not help, as it were unconsciously, drawing conclusions which, under the guise of objectivity, constituted a distinct philosophy.

To draw such conclusions is of particular importance in psychology, because the object of its study is the human person, an object itself capable of drawing conclusions, thinking, and of value judgments. Thus psychology, and particularly depth psychology, which is the science of the hidden motives of human behavior, plays its part in the philosophical thinking of our times. It is far better that it should play this part consciously than allow its influence to remain unrecognized (89).

In summation, it can be said that Catholic authors, taking their direction from the Magisterium, voice the following general concerns about Jung. First, what does Jung's projection of internal experience onto external impression mean? Some maintain that Jung never goes beyond the individual experience, that he never 'transcends' the unique and arrives at the universal. Others argue that his conception of the archetype grounds him in the collective metaphysical experience.

Catholic writers are in agreement with Jung that theology touches the roots of human life. But is theology able to do that only when it is mediated through psychology? Third, there is a general reluctance to accept the Jungian stress on the "inside" as opposed to

42

the "outside" of life. Fourth, there is a perplexing and sometimes hostile resentment to Jung's use of theological terms, particularly when their use seems to be twisted to meet his preconceived needs.

Finally, Catholics must question Jung's contention that knowledge rests not upon truth along, but upon error also. How Jung explains such an existential position is crucial to his acceptability in Catholic thought. As this study unfolds, that position and allied ones will be scrutinized.

Chapter II

All that I have learned has
led me step by step to an
unshakable conviction:
the conviction that God exists.
I only believe what I see,
and that eliminates faith.
I do not have faith in God...
I know that He exists.

"The Last Interview with Carl G. Jung,"
Opera-Mundi, Paris, 1961.

HUMAN KNOWLEDGE ABOUT GOD

In an interdisciplinary study a major problem centers around the selection of materials. There are a variety of schools and a host of opinions as to what the content and process of the discipline rightly involves. It is easy to become either immobilized by the complexities involved or to create an umbrella so wide that almost any view can find shelter under it.

A perusal of a few theological writings points up the problem. One author suggests that there are five operative theological models: orthodox, liberal, non-orthodox, radical and revisionist (90). Another author lists six formative factors in theology: experience, revelation, scripture, tradition, culture and reason (91). Several sociologists who have examined the theological structure say that its taxonomy should include the ideological, intellectual, sacramental, experiential and consequential. This pluralism is a major factor in this study's focus on the defined teachings of the Catholic Church and its commonly accepted tradition.

In psychology, the same situation prevails. There is the foundational series of classical psychologists, Freud, Jung, Adler and Rank. Many other schools of psychology flow from them. Some few have little to do with them. Others, such as the behaviorists, disavow the classical constructs as useful in changing most behavior. About its disciplinary problems, Jung says that there is a total chaos in psychology, so do not be so frightfully serious about psychological theories. For him, psychology is not a religious creed but a point of view, and when we are tolerant about differing viewpoints we may be able to understand each other.

Jung assess the situation as follows: "Some people have sexual trouble and others have other troubles. I have chiefly other troubles. You now have an idea of how I look at things" (92).

To show the potential complexities involved in a theological analysis one need look no further than its specified object, "God." It does seem that it is not entirely clear what it means to believe in God. Some take it to be the assent to the existence of a supreme being; some take it to be the adoption of certain affective states of dispositional attitudes; others understand it as the entrance into a specific form of life, with its own unique type of language and styles of ritual activity, which is not comprehensible in non-religious terms, or outside that form of life. Even those who take one important element of theistic belief to be that of assent, do not agree on the object of their assent. There are those who conceive God as a supreme person; those who conceive God as an impersonal absolute; those who conceive God as eternal and immutable, and those who conceive God as temporal and in constant change (93).

> My problem, Jung says, is to wrestle with the big monster of the historical past, the great snake of the centuries, the burden of the human mind, the problem of Christianity. It would be so much simpler if I knew nothing; but I know too much, through my ancestors and my own education. Other people are not worried by such problems and they do not care about the historical burdens Christianity has heaped upon us. But there are people who are concerned with the great battle between the present and the past or the future. It is a tremendous human problem (94).

To complicate matters further, both psychology and theology have a distinct relationship to a third discipline, philosophy. In the first chapter we saw the disdain that Jung had for certain views of philosophy. However, he does soften his view toward philosophy in a number of places. For instance, he writes,

> I believe there are as many psychologies as philosophies, for there is also no single philosophy, but many. I mention this for the reason that philosophy and psychology are linked by indissoluble bonds which are kept in being by the inter-relation of their subject matters. Psychology takes the

46

psyche for its subject, and philosophy --- to put it briefly, takes the world (95). Until recently psychology was a special brand of philosophy, but now we are coming to something which Nietzsche foresaw --- the rise of psychology in its own right, so much so that it is even threatening to swallow philosophy. (96).

For Jung, the inner resemblance between the two disciplines of philosophy and psychology consists in this, that both are systems of opinions about objects which cannot be fully experienced and therefore cannot be adequately comprehended by a purely empirical approach. Both fields of study thus encourage speculation, with the result that opinions are formed in such a variety and profusion that many volumes are needed to contain them all. Neither discipline can do without the other, and the one invariably furnishes the unspoken --- and generally unconscious --- assumptions of the other.

For centuries, Catholicism considered philosophy the "hand-maiden" of theology. Pius IX in 1862 explained the role of philosophy in theology,

> True and sound philosophy has its own most noble position, since it is the characteristic of such philosophy to search diligently into truth, and to cultivate and illustrate rightly and carefully human reason, darkened as it is by the guilt of the first man, but by no means extinct; and to perceive, to understand well, to advance the object of its cognition and many truths; and to demonstrate, vindicate and defend, by arguments sought from its own principles, many of those truths, such as the existence, nature, attributes of God which faith also proposes for our belief; and, in this way, to build

47

a road to those dogmas more correctly held by faith, and even to those more profound dogmas which can be perceived by faith alone at first, so that they may in some way be understood by reason (97).

Pius XI in 1923 lent the Church's support to the philosophy of Thomas Aquinas (98). Contrary to widespread opinion, the Pope did not give an exclusive endorsement to Thomism. The directive states:

> Naturally among lovers of St. Thomas, such as all the sons of the Church who are concerned with the highest studies should be, we desire that there exist that honorable rivalry with just freedom from which studies make progress, but no detraction which is not favorable to truth and which serves only to break the bonds of charity. Therefore, let whatever is prescribed in the Code of Canon Law be sacred to each one of them, that 'the professors may carry on the study of rational philosophy and of theology and the instruction of their students in these disciplines according to the method, doctrines and principles of the Angelic Doctor, and may hold them sacred,' and that all so conduct themselves according to this norm as to be truly able to call him that master. 'But let not some exact from others anything more than this which the Church, the mistress and mother of all demands of all; for in those matters about which there is wont to be varied opinions among teachers of higher distinction among our Catholic schools no one is to be prevented from following the opinion which seems to him the more probable.'

Though there is no resolution to the pluralism of the psychological and theological worlds, it is necessary to allude to its existence. This study is committed to two specific systematic formulations. Though aware of other options and other interpretations, this

48

examination is limited to the formal articulation of an orthodox Jungian and a Catholic magisterial viewpoint.

For both of these systems, the question of how we arrive at our knowledge of God is of significance. We are, by our earlier methodological stipulations, limited to a natural study of that process, granted that it is feasible. Though the focus is on "God" in this first presupposition, we may include other religious elements directly related to God.

I. The First Presupposition: Human Knowledge about God

A. The Catholic View: The human mind, independently of the historic revelation and its acceptance by faith, basing itself solely on the data provided by our natural human faculties, can reach certain conclusions about God.

There is general agreement that St. Anselm, following St. Augustine, found the best and briefest formula which covers all that theology sets out to do, and yet must always fail to do. The role of theology, for them, is to help us understand what it is that we already believe ("intelligere quod credimus.") Theology is, then, the attempt to understand, to make intelligible, what we accept by faith. Whatever can justly claim to come under that heading, to that extent pertains to theology.

49

It has traditionally been difficult for Catholic theology to discern what constitutes its parameters because ultimately, according to Catholic theology, all of reality has some reference to God. Religious experience is embedded in general experience; it may be distinguished but it is not separated.

Further, from the Catholic perspective, theology's understanding is at least partially mediated through other disciplines. Without that mediation every theological expression would be isolated from human experience. For example, a serious theological study of the human person would be incomplete without examining what history, anthropology, sociology, psychology, and philosophy might contribute.

It is in this setting that Catholic systematic thought makes a distinction between natural and supernatural theology. Supernatural theology is the scientific exposition of the truths about God derived from what God says about Himself. Supernatural theology is excluded from this study of selected presuppositions. Natural theology is the scientific exposition of the truths concerning God, insofar as these can be known by natural reason. This type of theology is related to, and some say, si the culmination of philosophy

Catholic Theology has always been fairly optimistic about the condition of the human person, in spite of the results of original sin. Deprivation, not depravity, sums up sinful human character. The 'wounding of nature' is not to be conceived, with the Reformers and the Jansenists, as the complete corruption of human nature. In the condition of original sin, man possesses the ability of knowing natural religious truths and of performing natural morally good actions (99). The I Vatican Council teaches that man, with his natural power of cognition, can with certainty know the existence of God. The Council of Trent teaches that free will was not lost or extinguished by the fall of Adam.

Of course, natural theology is idle talk for those who maintain that the mind of the human person is so limited and infected with sin that the quest for truth is vitiated from the beginning. For these Christians, faith, the response to God's advent in Christ, is the beginning and the end of knowledge.

The hope of a productive dialogue between the Catholic and the Jungian systems rests on avoiding any confrontation of supernatural and natural truths. Because of Jung's sympathetic disposition to natural theology, we can examine certain Catholic theological positions which have their correlates in Jungian psychology. Without a natural theology our endeavor would be stillborn, since we would simply be subjecting Jung's position to an authoritative scrutiny from a solely revealed religion.

The truths of natural theology have not necessarily been revealed but are intrinsically associated with a revealed truth. This includes those philosophic truths which are presuppositions of the acts of Faith (knowledge of the supersensual, possibility of proofs of God, the spirituality of the soul, the freedom of the will), or philosophic concepts, in terms of which dogma is promulgated (person, substance, transubstantiation, etc.). The Church reserves to itself both the right and the duty, for the protection of the heritage of Faith, or proscribing philosophic teachings which directly or indirectly endanger dogma.

The I Vatican Council defined that God, ourCreator and Lord, can be known with certainty, by the natural light of reason from created things. The definition stresses the following points: a) The object of our knowing (100) is the one true God, our Creator and Lord, and therefore an extra-mundane, personal God; b) The subjective principle of knowledge is natural reason in the condition of fallen nature; c) The means of knowledge are created things; d) The knowledge is from its nature and manner a knowledge of certitude; e) Such knowledge of God is possible, but it is not the only way of knowing him.

The early Fathers of the Church developed the proofs of God along two lines. While some preferred the cosmological proofs which proceed from external experience, others preferred the psychological proofs which flow from inner experience. Many theologians have taught that the idea of God is not acquired by deductive thing from the world of experience, but is innate in man.

Certainly many of the Fathers, for example, St. Justin (Apol. II, 6) and St. Clement of Alexandria (Strom. V. 14, 133 F) characterized the knowledge of God as "automatic," "not learned," "automatically learned," "implanted," "self-taught," or as a "gift of the soul" (Tertullian, Adv. Marc 1, 10). St. John of Damascus says, "The Knowledge of the existence of God is implanted (by Him) in all in their nature." (De Fide orth. I.I.).

But as the same Fathers teach that we must win the knowledge of God from the contemplation of nature, therefore, according to their conception, what is innate is not the idea of God as such, but the ability easily and to a certain extent spontaneously to know the existence of God from his works. St. Thomas in Boethium De Trinitate, a. I. A. 3 and 6 states, "The knowledge of Him is said to be innate in us insofar as we can easily know the existence of God by means of principles which are innate in us."

In the Catholic schema natural theology plays a very useful and perhaps even indispensable part in the whole theological enterprise. It links the theologian's world with the world of ordinary experience (101), or, to put the same thing in another way, it shows the connection between theological discourse and everyday discourse. It provides a foundation for theology and prepares the Catholic for the reception of revealed truths.

B. The Jungian View: God is not a transcendent reality of which we may achieve some knowledge by means of natural reason, but rather an "archetype" of a basic tendency in human nature.

Kantianism is listed in Ott's Fundamentals of Catholic Dogma as an erroneous position denying the natural know-ability of God. While Kant in his pre-critical period recognized the possibility of the proofs of God, and even developed the ideological proof of God (cf. the article published in 1763: "The only possible ground of proof for a demonstration of the existence of God"), in his critical period he denied the validity of all proofs of God (cf. the Critique of Pure Reason which appeared in 1781).

According to Kant, the only object of theoretical reason is the world of phenomena; the supersensual is withdrawn from it. The validity of the principle of causality is limited to things perceptible to the senses. In order to refute the individual proofs of God's existence, Kant sought to show that they all go back to the ontological argument by deriving from the concept of the Supreme Reality its factual existence. Nevertheless, Kant believed in the existence of God and designated this belief the postulate of practical reason.

Kant's philosophy exercised a decisive influence on certain theologies. From the standpoint of the Kantian doctrine of cognition they rejected the rational foundation of religion, and with it the intellectual proofs of the existence of God. They taught that religious truths must be perceived, not by reason, but through religious feeling, which affirms the existence of God and by which we live in God. They claimed that it is on this subjective religious experience that faith is founded.

Though Jung is ambivalent about his philosophical affiliations there is no question that he is Kantian in his outlook. He says that the existence of God is once and for all an unanswerable question. The majority of people have been talking of gods for eons and will still be talking of them eons hence. According to Jung, no matter how beautiful and perfect the human person may believe reason to be, we can always be certain that it is only one of the possible mental functions, and covers only that one side of the phenomenal world which corresponds to it.

Jung interprets the experience of the self as an experience of God, with the aid of metaphysical concepts and terms which he adapts to the methodical level of psychic experience. How does he justify this? "A new philosophy of life must reject all superstitious belief in its objective validity, it must be able to admit that it is only a picture that we paint to please our own soul and not a magic formula with which we posit objective things" (102). According to this, philosophy of life is merely an extension and deepening of consciousness. This means, however, that all our own thinking, knowing, and feeling about the meaning of our existence is mere psychology.

In The Secret of the Golden Flower, Jung says that it is impossible to understand metaphysically; it can only be done psychologically. "The fact that I restrict myself to what can be psychologically experienced and repudiate the metaphysical does not mean, as anyone with insight can understand, a gesture of scepticism or agnosticism pointed against faith or trust in higher powers, but which I intend to say is approximately the same thing as Kant meant when he called "das Ding an sich" (the thing in itself) a purely negative borderline concept" (103). For Jung, every statement about the metaphysical ought to be avoided because it is invariably a laughable presumption on the part of the human mind, unconscious of its limitations.

For Jung, the object of faith lies not in the existence of an infinite God outside man, but rather in the contents of the collective unconscious as they reveal themselves in consciousness as the symbol of an incomprehensible content. For Jung the important factor is the image of God, and when he speaks, he speaks of a psychological image, for psychology must deal with these images only insofar as they come under our experience. But this, he insists, has nothing to do with God as such (104).

"How could any sane man suppose he could displace God or do anything whatever to him? I am not so mad that I should be suspected of intending to create a substitute for God. How could any man replace God?... The best I can do is to have a divine image, and I am not the idiot to say that the image I behold in the mirror is my real, living self" (105).

It is therefore the fault of the contamination of the object and image that people can make no conceptual distinction between "God" and "God-image," and therefore, Jung says, think that when one speaks of the God-image one is speaking of God and offering theological explanations. Psychology cannot demand the hypostatization of the God-image, but it does have to reckon with the existence of a God-image in the same way it reckons with instinct. What God is in Himself remains a question outside the competence of all psychology (106).

Religion is directly connected with the contents of the collective unconscious. But how is it possible to know these contents? These contents are known through revelation (107). This is not the Christian revelation, which presupposes the manifestation of a transcendent God, existing outside the human person and outside the universe. No, the Jungian revelation is a personal and unique phenomenon which everybody can experience if properly disposed. This unique experience manifests the secrets hidden in the unconscious, because "revelation is an unveiling of the depths of the human soul, a laying bare; hence it is an essentially psychological event" (108).

In other words, "religion is a careful and scrupulous observation of what Rudolf Otto aptly termed the numinosum; that is, a dynamic agency or effect not caused by an arbitrary act of the will . . . it seizes and controls the human subject who is always rather its victim than its creator" (109). Religious experience is so powerful that it produces deep psychological effects, even transformation of human personalities, and alteration of consciousness (110).

The root of religion is revelation, so the nature of religion --- and, as a consequence, of God --- will depend, psychologically speaking, on the nature of the experience of the numinous. It will depend also on the nature of the contents of the collective unconscious which erupts into consciousness as revelation opens the treasures stored in the depths of the human psyche. The collective unconscious reveals itself as full of power, with a sense of mystery and strong feelings. This kind of human experience Jung calls religious experience and the factors producing it are the archetypes of the collective unconscious.

The archetypal activity results in religious symbols that have a distinctly "revelatory" character. Spontaneous products of unconscious psychic activity, they are anything rather than thought up. On the contrary, in the course of the millenia, they have

58

developed, plant-like, as natural manifestations of the human psyche.

Even today, Jung tells us, we see in individuals the spontaneous genesis of genuine and valid religious symbols, springing from the unconscious like flowers of a strange species, while consciousness stands aside perplexed, not knowing what to make of such creations. It can be ascertained without too much difficulty that in form and content those individual symbols arise from the same unconscious mind or "spirit" (or whatever it may be called) as the great religions of mankind.

At all events, Jung maintains that experience shows that religions are in no sense conscious constructions, but that they arise from the natural life of the unconscious psyche and somehow give adequate expression to it. This explains their universal distribution and their enormous influence on humanity throughout history, which would be incomprehensible if religious symbols were not at the very least truths of our psychological nature.

C. Human Knowledge About God: Catholicism and Jung in Dialogue.

There are seven serious points of contention in the first presupposition. Theology might formulate these controversial points in the form of charges. They are listed below with their Jungian response (111).

1) In asserting that religion is a living relation to psychic events which do not depend upon consciousness, Jung is making a statement outside the bounds of psychology as a science. Jung replies, "The psychic events which do not depend upon consciousness are those which depend upon the unconscious side of personality, still a proposition within the scientific domain" (112).

2) Although Jung acknowledges he can say nothing as a scientist about God outside of experience, he states that God does not exist independently of the human subject. Jung replies, "Insofar as God has any existence which affects the individual subject, this existence is found in psychic experience, usually as an unconscious content of this experience" (113).

3) Jung does not distinguish between psychic statements to which a superpsychic reality corresponds and those to which none corresponds. Jung replies, "Whether a superpsychic reality corresponds to man's metaphysical beliefs is a question outside of science. Where beliefs have a basis in psychic events, this basis is demonstrable by science" (114).

4) Jung says that men make their own images of God. Jung replies, "The human psyche generates imagery of God, but this does not

mean mere ideas or copies. Rather the imagery is the concrete experience by which spiritual motivation expresses itself. This is an experience of motivation in oneself and in others" (115).

5) Despite Jung's claim of sympathy toward religion approached by faith, he asserts that it is to psychic experience which the individual must turn for religion truth. Jung replies, "People are to be encouraged to base their religious beliefs upon psychic facts, but this does not exclude the importance to the individual of faith held on other grounds" (116).

6) Jung declares that metaphysical statements are expressions of the soul, which would deny philosophy the basis for truth independent of the individual's own psychological processes. Jung replies, "Although philosophical beliefs are generated by the functioning of personality and answer personality needs, the origin of these beliefs in psychic functioning does not define the question of their truth or falsity (117)."

7) Jung fails to demonstrate an essentially personal relationship of man to a God who is experienced. Jung replies, "The human psyche often generates archetypes of a personal deity, Jesus for example, to whom the individual experiences a personal relationship" (118).

In an earlier statement I maintained that Jung's "modernist" tendencies creates serious problems in establishing some kind of rapprochement with magisterial thinking. Because of its importance to the dialogue between Jung and Catholicism, it is necessary to avert to Jung's at least implicit attachment to modernism.

Pius X summarizes some of the Church's problems with Jung when he states the case against Modernism.

> Now to begin with the philosopher, the Modernists place the foundation of their religious philosophy in that doctrine which is commonly called agnosticism (119). Perforce, then, human reason is entirely restricted to phenomena, namely, things that appear, and that appearance by which they appear; it has neither the right nor the power to transgress the limits of the same.
>
> Modernism holds that religion is to be sought within man himself; and since religion is a form of life, it is to be found entirely within the life of man. From this is asserted the principle of religious immanence.
>
> Moreover, of every vital phenomenon, to which it has just been said religion belongs, the first actuation, as it were, is to be sought in a certain need or impulsion; but if we speak more specifically of life, the beginnings are to be posited in a kind of motion of the heart, which is called a sense. Therefore, since God is the object of religion, it must be concluded absolutely that faith, which is the beginning and the foundation of any religion, must be located in some innermost sense, which has its beginnings in a need for the divine. Moreover, this need for the divine, since it is felt only in certain special surroundings, cannot of itself pertain to the realm of consciousness, but it remains hidden at first beneath consciousness or, as they say with a word borrowed from modern philosophy, in the subconsciousness, where, too its roots remain hidden and undetected.

Someone perhaps will ask in what way does this need of the divine, which man himself perceives within himself, finally evolve into religion? To this the Modernists reply, 'Science and history are included within a twofold boundary; one external, that is the visible world, the other internal, which is consciousness. When they have reached one or the other, they are unable to proceed further, for beyond these boundaries is the unknowable. In the presence of this unknowable, whether this be outside man and beyond the perceptible world of nature, or lies concealed within the subconscious, the need of the divine in a soul prone to religion, according to the tenets of fideism, with no judgment of the mind anticipating, excites a certain peculiar sense; but this sense has the divine reality itself, not only as its object but also as its intrinsic cause implicated within itself, and somehow unites man with God. This sense, moreover, is what the Modernists call by the name of faith, and is for them the beginning of religion.

Any number of Catholic thinkers find Jung's exposition of religion that of an agnostic. It is a short step to finding him a modernist. At best, Jung presents the controversial Janus-sided explanations that often allow opponents to quote him with equal confidence. Essentialist philosophers speak fondly of his essentially conservative view of nature and its development (120). Existentially oriented philosophers are impressed with the direction and movement that pervade Jung's thought. For them, Jung worked with an implicit process conception of reality and with a theology of divine relativity.

If Catholicism were to examine Jung from the perspective of method and object, it is the object that presents the greater difficulty. For example, the history, nature and concrete life of Christ is for Jung of very little importance. Why? Because Jung's approach to Christ is psychological, neither theological nor metaphysical. Christ personifies the collective expectations of the unconscious because lived the concrete, personal life which, in all essential features, had at the same time archetypal character. Since the archetypes of the collective unconscious are not personal, but universal, the life of Christ symbolizes the eternal life of the species, and thus what happens in the life of Christ happens always and everywhere. Here lies the central idea of Jung's approach to Christ: the life of Christ is a perfect expression of the needs of the archetype of the unconscious.

But the magisterial position maintains that natural theology cannot encompass the Christ question since He is a product of supernatural revelation. The strong objection to Jung's thought about Christ does not affect the possible compatibility of the two systems on the natural level. Conversely, Jung may use the Christ example without damaging his own credibility. Christ is simply the existing archetype that illustrates the point he is making.

Some charge that the most glaring difficulties that Jung's psychology presents are based on the fact that many of his implications are stated in metaphoric rather than literal language. This is not a damaging charge insofar as magisterial theology is concerned. Victor white points out for instance, that for Aquinas it is almost axiomatic that the different human sciences and disciplines are to be distinguished, not necessarily by different subject matter or fields of inquiry, but by the different ways in which the subject matter can be rendered knowable by and to the human mind (121). It is no scandal to Aquinas that the selfsame 'God' whom the believer acknowledges by faith in revelation could also be the legitimate object of purely rational inquiry.

> The viewpoint and method of the theologian who tires to 'understand what he believes,' and of the empiricist or rational thinker who tries to draw the consequences from what he observes, will differ widely; so also may their conclusion. If they should appear to conflict, loyalty to truth will require of each that he should verify and check his own processes, and attempt to understand those of the other, and to see where misunderstandings and mistakes may have arisen. (122).

The Pyschiatrist, Braceland, suggests,

> It is too easily forgotten that most of the terms used in psychology and psychiatry are metaphors and do not directly indicate the nature of that to which they refer. Through frequent use they come to be taken as denotations of reality. Thus, it is customary to refer to certain schools of psychotherapy by the common name of 'depth psychology' and so to speak of 'depths' or 'layers' of the human mind . . . However much the metaphor of depth may suggest, it remains a metaphor, and one is not entitled to speak of the 'layers' of the mind as realities (123).

But, as a matter of fact, the base of all metaphors is man's common daily experience of nature and society. This experience provides him with the raw materials for all of his imaginative extensions of

65

language and experience. What other source could there be? What the human mind does is to take striking or significant aspects of this experience and use them to express or articulate new or unique facets of human experience. Thus a metaphor --- any metaphor --- is an image that has been stretched or extended for this purpose.

Even theological models do not purport to provide exact pictures of the realities they disclose. Theological disclosure models, like the religious symbols upon which they reflect, in Reinhold Niebuhr's famous phrase, should be taken seriously but not literally. Theologies do not, or should not, claim to provide pictures of the realities they describe - God, humanity and world; they can be shown to disclose such realities with varying degrees of adequacy.

Theology works out of symbols to symbols, articulating and structuring the timeless truth of Christ to the particular temporal human situation. Depth psychology itself is a symbolic system expressing interpretations of human existence (124). The necessity to produce symbols is the psychological basis of the religious function. In producing images of God, the psyche tries to express its subjective relation to the source of life and to meaning itself. The symbols that reconcile psychic polarities build up an inner psychic unity that interpenetrates with the unity posited and perceived in God.

The importance of symbols and the religious function for the nature of one's world suggests that theology, too, is a symbolic form of perception. Statements about God, then, must be understood as formative models of reality by whose agency God becomes an object for apprehension. Hence, theology is like an art form; it often consists of picture -making and myth-creating. In criticizing theologies one must consider the images used in terms of their ability to organize experience and, indeed, make it possible.

Because an image speaks to the whole person --- his mind, heart, senses, experience and imagination --- it engages him more fully than does a mental concept. Hence, implicit in the symbolic mode is a relational aspect; we are touched and we respond. We are in the midst, not abstracted; this anchors our, by now, almost autonomous conceptualizing faculties in a total human response (125). Theology is thereby spared its usual reception as a theoretical system addressed only to the intellectually adept and becomes, like psychology, a world of total human experience, accessible to all sorts of human beings. Jung criticizes the theologians' failure to deal with symbols in his words to Upton Sinclair, "It is tragic that science and its philosophy discourage the individual and that theology resists every reasonable attempt at an understanding of its symbols. They call their creed 'symbolism' but they refuse to call their 'truth' symbolic, yet if it is anything, it is . . . symbolism and therefore capable of reinterpretation" (126).

The significance of the unconscious mind of the human race for religion or for any field of endeavor can hardly be overestimated.

The unconscious realm is the vast reservoir of new ideas, except those which come directly from new experiences of the external world. The method of experimentation in science furnishes fresh data, but the implications which can be abstracted from the data of either the external or internal world seems a limitless capacity of the human mind. The unconscious side of personality contains much more than the unfulfilled ideas of which people are aware and to which they aspire. It contains countless ideals, plans, and possibilities as yet unthought of. This inexhaustible capacity of the unconscious mind seems to be the basis for the infinite possibilities traditionally ascribed to God.

Some prominent Catholic writers are in agreement with Jung's assessment of contemporary life. Leslie Dewart says,

> The contemporary crisis of man I take to be an essentially 'religious' one. Religion in general, and belief in God in particular, have been deeply affected by the evolution of man, for this evolution has already brought about a change in the very nature of 'religious' belief. To put it conversely, if we cannot readily identify and diagnose the problem of man in the twentieth century, much of the difficulty is that we do not recognize it as a religious problem --- precisely because the common idea of religion is derived from what religion used to be in the past, rather than what it must be today, given the changes that have already affected the nature of man (127).

It is the theologian's experience that contemporary religious scepticism is due less to a widespread belief that the gospels and creeds are positively untrue, than to the widespread feeling that they are irrelevant. It is precisely the relevance of faith and practice to the needs and workings of the human psyche that Jung's psychology appears to have rediscovered, and to be subjecting to methodical study. Jung's insistence on dealing with religious phenomena and affirmations within a psychological from of reference, that is to say, one in which the individual and his needs are the prime and only consideration, has a valuable contribution to make to the understanding of the relevance of religion.

Chapter III

Robert: How do you mean, voices?
Joan: I heard voices telling me what to do.
Robert: They come from your imagination.
Joan: Of course, that is how the messages of
God comes to us.

George Bernard Shaw, St. Joan

CHAPTER III

RELIGIOUS EXPERIENCE

Knowledge of God is interwoven with the experience of God. As I have already mentioned, Jung frequently speaks of the "experience" of God. For Catholics, this "experience" usually translates into "knowledge" of God. Does the same process work for the Jungians? Can Catholic "knowledge" be translated into Jungian "experience?" This part of the discussion deals with experience and attempts to answer some of the questions that arise from both the Jungian and the Catholic use of the term.

Are we in the West at the point of rediscovering our theological heritage through the psychological sciences? Does the emergence of the psychological and psychotherapeutic disciplines signify the appearance of an outsider, or are these disciplines really the insider we have so long neglected, but for which we have nevertheless been responsible all along? In what sense is faith a developmental phenomenon, continuous with those stages, tasks sequences, and the like, of which psychology so often speaks? Are we to think of faith more in terms of its object, thereby assigning the task of understanding it to the systematic theologian?

Perhaps one of the most significant developments --- certainly one of the most surprising --- in the history of Christian belief is the emergence in recent times of a not inconsiderable number of Christian believers, particularly among professional theologians, who share in many respects the very objections which in the past have moved many to agnosticism and atheism (128). Yet, though persuaded of the fundamental moral validity of the motives which in the past have led to disbelief, these Christians do not themselves disbelieve. The reason is that they are also convinced that the choice between belief and disbelief in the traditional concept of God is not a legitimate alternative.

They think instead that the concept of God must, like every other, undergo development as we grow and mature. They believe that, as human consciousness evolves, new possibilities for the evolution of the Christian faith are opened up. Their problem is, therefore, now how to defend the traditional concept of God against contemporary experience but, on the contrary, how to take advantage of the growth of human experience in order to improve upon their concept of God.

Experience is one of the most enigmatic of concept (129). It is ordinarily taken to be a source or special form of our knowledge, deriving from the immediate reception of the given or of the impression, in contrast to discursive thought, mere concepts, authoritatively accepted opinions or historical tradition. When experience presents itself, its presence means a special kind of supreme certitude of irrefutable evidence. Since the human spirit is primarily "in potency," and hence needs the knowledge which takes in what it perceives, human knowledge and experience are profoundly identical.

There can be no doubt of the legitimacy and importance of the notion of experience in theology. But for the Catholic the following stipulations belong to a consideration of religious experience: 1) The significance for salvation (130) which is implied in a theological truth can only be adequately demonstrated when the person's receptivity for such truth has been investigated. The truth of God is also the truth of our existence and its meaning. 2) The full nature of religion and faith cannot be based theologically merely on experience and certainty, since the reality of faith which is offered and bestowed in grace is a deed of God which penetrates and embraces us more thoroughly than anything which can be reflected in concrete experience. Experience is by the nature of things never adequately rendered.

Experience is variously perceived, but it seems to incorporate four potential meanings --- verification, knowledge drawn from life, experimentation, and habitual knowledge (131). The common element is an immediate knowledge of concrete things, and ultimately, the word experience suggests concrete knowledge and knowledge united to life. Experience can be regarded as a search for truth. This kind of experience is governed by and directed towards discovery, proof, verification, and it involves a series of steps which, as a result of an inquiry conducted at different levels, end in the apprehension, formulation and proof of a new truth.

But "experience" can also denote the grasp of a reality (132). In this sense every experience is something that is received. It is the consciousness of a given reality; not a search for truth, but the experienced presence of a reality; not a journey, but possession. This kind of experience lies at the very heart of a particular order of realities or values. And when the reality in question is spiritual, and necessarily complex, experience means the possession, the consciousness of, the deepening insight into, a structured reality (133). It can then be defined as the act or series of acts involved in apprehending an object or realizing a presence, the consciousness of an experienced structure. In short, it is in the first place an activity involving contract and, ultimately, communion.

There are few more deeply human problems than the problem of religious experience. One would therefore expect this problem and the idea on which it centers to have been studied frequently, at length, and in systematic detail. But such is not the case. It is at the juncture of experience that Jung and Catholicism search for a penetration of the religious and the psychological. In modern times William James' The Varieties of Religious Experience provides the point of departure (134).

Jean Moroux provides a popular Catholic interpretation of religious experience in his analysis of the possible levels of experience. He suggests three levels; empirical, experimental, and experiential. The empirical includes experience that remains uncriticized, which is endured but not brought out into the open; it constitutes the elements of experience rather than experience proper.

Experimental experience involves the conscious, intentional level, pivoting also around particular elements. But these elements can be measured; these are aroused, manipulated, and coordinated, and ultimately constructed into the world of science. For Moroux the experiential level is that at which an experience is understood in its personal totality, with all its structural elements, all its motivating principles. It is built up and grasped in a clear consciousness that is in full possession of itself, and in generous, self-giving love --- in short, a personal experience in the fullest sense of the word. For Moroux, as for many others, religious experience is situated beyond the realms of the empiric and the experimental and entirely in the field of the experiential.

Jung tells us that since the psyche is an irrational datum and cannot, in according with the old picture, be equated with a more or less divine reason, it should not surprise us if in the course of psychological experience we come across, with extreme frequency, processes and happenings which run counter to our rational expectations and are therefore rejected by the rationalistic attitude of our conscious mind (135). Such an attitude is naturally not very skilled at psychological observation because it is in the highest degree unscientific. We must not attempt to tell nature what to do if we want to observe her operations undisturbed.

There is religious experience wherever there is living contact with God (136). In this sense, all religions admit a certain form of religious experience, because the personal movement towards God, which is essential to all religions, implies the quest of this very contact. Religious experience is therefore a normal element of the life of religion, and may show itself in various forms, crude or discreet, distorted or well-balanced. Hence it can be found among the "primitives" as well as among the civilized.

But this experience is extremely polyvalent. In spite of appearance, there is no such thing as pure religious experience. It always implies moral, metaphysical, and mystical elements embedded in a historical process and institutions. It is known in the perspective of a certain way of thought, worship and life, and is channeled by a whole series of mediators; the religious person must always respond to a tradition (ethnic, cultural or religious), if only to deny it.

According to Jung, "legitimate" faith must always rest on experience (137). There is, however, another kind of faith which rests exclusively on the authority of tradition. This kind of faith could also be called "legitimate," since the power of tradition embodies an experience whose importance for the continuity of culture is beyond question. Though Jung is ambivalent about the subject, he generally suggests that the Protestant experiences God "directly," while the Catholic relates to God through a Church which has interjected itself between God and the person (138). Though the first is a more demanding experience, the latter provides a sense of security (139).

In a tradition-bound faith there is always the danger of mere habit intervening --- it may so easily degenerate into spiritual inertia and a thoughtless compliance which, if persisted in, threatens stagnation and cultural regression. This mechanical dependence goes hand in hand with a psychic regression to infantilism. The traditional contents gradually lose their real meaning and are only believed in as formalities, without this belief having any influence on the conduct of life. There is no longer a living power behind it.

The much-vaunted "child-likeness" of faith only makes sense when the feeling behind the experience is still alive. If it gets lost, faith is only another word for habitual, infantile dependence, which takes the place of, and actually prevents, the struggle for deeper understanding (140). This seems to be the position we have reached today. Since faith revolves around those central and perennially important "dominant ideas" which alone gives life a meaning, the prime task of the psychotherapist must be to understand the symbols anew, and thus to understand the unconscious, compensatory striving of his patient for an attitude that reflects the totality of the psyche.

II. The Second Presupposition: Religious Experience

A. The Catholic View: Experience is of an experiential type, complex in structure, and it puts in their proper order all the levels of human nature. It is composed of the network of relationships by which the person grasps himself in contact with God.

We return again to a basic premise: Jung is a tacit modernist. That being the case, there is a considerable amount of magisterial literature directed to those who hold such a position, knowingly or not. This literature can be used to study Jung though it is not directed to him.

We turn again to Pius X to set the Catholic milieu for experience. By reacting to modernism, Pius not only outlines the failings of modernism, but he also suggests what components might go to making up the Catholic religious experience. Certainly Jung is not an unbridled modernist. He offers many nuances to modernism's basic tenets.

> Now if, on advancing to the believer, one wishes to know how he is distinguished from the philosopher among the modernists, this must be observed that, although the philosopher admits the reality of the divine as the object of faith, yet this reality is not found by him anywhere except in the heart of the believer, since it is the object of sense and of affirmation, and so does not exceed the confines of phenomena; furthermore, whether that reality exists in itself outside that sense and affirmation, the philosopher passes over and neglects.

> On the other hand for the modernist believer it is established and certain that the reality of the divine definitely exists in itself, and certainly does not depend on the believer. But if you ask on what then the assertion of the believer rests, they will reply: in the personal experience of every man. In this affirmation, while they break with the rationalists, to be sure, yet they fall in with the opinion of Protestants and pseudomystics. For they explain the subject as follows: that in the religious sense a kind of intuition of the heart is to be recognized, by which man directly attains the reality of God, and draws from it such conviction of the existence of God and of the action of God both within and without man, that it surpasses by far all conviction that can be sought from science.

> They establish, then, a true experience and one superior to any rational experience. If anyone, such as the rationalists, deny this, they say that this arises from the fact that he is

unwilling to establish himself in the moral state which is required to produce the experience. Furthermore, this experience, when anyone has attained it, properly and truly makes a believer --- how far we are here from Catholic teachings (141).

We have already seen the extensive role that experience generates in the process of natural theology. In the condemnation of modernism Pius points out the negative components of religious experience. But he does not explicitly address himself to the positive Catholic qualities and it is to those that we must turn.

We know God and His plan for us ultimately to the extent that He has revealed Himself and acted in history. One must know the person, the scene and state of history, to know what this revelation and action are. We must know the terms of a statement before we can understand it and further its directives. This may be put another way. We cannot know God directly, as He is in Himself. Christian tradition is firm on this. But we can know Him and His designs from His relation to us. We must first understand ourselves, however, before we can understand this relation. To know what the Redeemer and Redemption are, we must know who and what are redeemed.

The fundamental concepts, attitudes and modes of experience that define human nature have not remained the same with the passage of time (142). The doctrines of faith must change, not because faith was originally deficient or mistaken, but, on the contrary, because to the extent that it was creative and true it has contributed to the development of human consciousness. Thus, the doctrines of faith must change because the nature of faith so requires; that is, the doctrines of faith must change because the human experience which faith makes meaningful and worthwhile does itself change --- not least radically of all to the very degree that faith is an effective factor in the evolution of the person.

It is clear that one cannot just say that God is wholly transcendent, meaning that he is totally and in every respect beyond the physical universe; for then one would have no way of knowing his existence. One must begin from some experienced features of the world, and assert that, in them, one has knowledge of a reality which is also transcendent in its being. One characterizes God in the way which evokes an appropriate attitude in the person, not in the way which describes his inner being most correctly. Naturally, if one's concepts do evoke an appropriate human response, one will say that they are not misleading; they do not describe God incorrectly, by comparison with a possibly more correct description. Yet the truth is that God cannot be described at all; so all one can ask is that one's concepts of God enable one to react to him and to one's experience at large in the right way.

Many in our culture have come to think --- or perhaps they have simply come to feel instinctively --- that to believe in any God unconditionally and uncritically regardless of what it should commit us to think and do, should offend the sense of propriety of any reasonable person of mature character and delicate moral sensibility. It is not that one should believe only in a God without mystery, a God totally open to human inspection. But one may not with a clear conscience believe in a God who is not consonant with human experience, and least of all in a God who outrages our moral sense. This kind of God one believes in is, after all, the best measure of the depth of one's self-understanding and moral insight (143).

To make religious belief depend on verification might seem to make it essentially a matter of hypothesis, revisable in the light of further discoveries and thus never attaining the full certainty of unshakeable commitment. So it seems that, either Christianity consists in a total commitment which has nothing to do with historical fact or the nature of the universe, or it is belief which is disproportionate to the evidence, and is at best speculative and probabilistic.

It is possible that a way may be found which allows an approach to reality which, though cognitive, yet depends essentially upon imaginative symbolization and creative personal response to what is apprehended. The very nature of such an approach would rule out the possibility of a detached experimental concern, which would be necessarily manipulative rather than responsive and interactive.

One may then say that the basic starting point of religious belief is a type of revelatory experience, in which a seeker seems to discern a non-material reality --- it may be in events in his life, in the forces of nature, or in the silence of inner contemplation --- which brings him to fulfillment, by disclosing a greater value and significance, by putting things in a new perspective. Such experiences may give a clue to the overall pattern of life, the meaning of life, and so be the center-points for a new vision and life.

The religious believer should say that the concepts which are distinctive of religion, and which, for a theist, are grouped around the concept of God, express a distinctive method of approach to reality, which can be cultivated or ignored by the individual. And they can, used properly, provide a unique means of releasing the imagination to see situations in a new and deeper light. Religion provides a way of communication with the inner realities of what is encountered in experience. And two important things must not be forgotten here: first, that this communication can be achieved only by an active and creative use of the imagination; and, second, that experienced reality is wider than empirical, or purely sensory experience.

It is important to see that belief is not a passive acceptance of creeds or dogmas, but an individual creative activity, in which the images of faith, which evoke an clarify specific human moods and reactions, are re-worked and explored, as one's own experience and thinking develops (144). It is in religious belief that every individual is capable of finding depths of creativity which can and should enrich and extend his own reactions to the world. To study the language of a religious faith, in its context of ritual and cultural action, is to learn the way to the imaginative apprehension of the world which distinguishes that faith, and within which believers find the pattern of their experience and action becoming clear to them.

For the Catholic, faith is the ultimate product of religious experience. Pius IX states that faith is simply related to supernatural experience (145). Since man is wholly dependent on God as his Creator and Lord, and since created reason is completely subject to uncreated truth, we are bound by faith to give full obedience of intellect and will to God who reveals. But the Catholic Church professes that this faith, which 'is the beginning of human salvation,' is a supernatural virtue by which we, with the aid and inspiration of the grace of God, believe that the things revealed by Him are true, not because the intrinsic truth of the revealed things has been perceived by the natural light of reason, but because of the authority of God himself who reveals them, who can neither deceive nor be deceived. For, "faith is," as the Apostle testifies, "the substance of things to be hoped for, the evidence of things that appear not."

As Dewart points out, if faith is assent to a truth revealed by God, an assent given on the basis of God's authority rather than on the basis of our vision of the truth, then the formulation or conceptualization of the truths of human faith lies outside the realm of human experience. In this view, the truth of faith is literally a divine truth, for it is the truth of God's own understanding of Himself; it is the truth of God Himself transplanted into a human mind which can but mindlessly hold it, nodding to itself that, whatever it may mean, it holds within itself a divinely guaranteed truth (146).

Faith is the person's self-understanding, but precisely as relative to a transcendent reality beyond himself. Faith is, therefore, on the one hand, the manifestation of the person to self, in the sense that the person's consciousness of existence defines him to himself as an essentially religious animal. On the other hand, when consciousness manifests the person to himself, it manifests him as a reality who in his very being, and even in his consciousness of being, is relative to reality which is not measured by the person's being, or even by the person's consciousness of being.

Faith is not an imperfect sort of everyday consciousness about perfect and extraordinary matters, but it is a distinct dimension of human experience which affects the person's consciousness of all things. Religious faith is not unlike human love, whose constant not infrequently leads to logical inconsistencies. If religious faith is transforming, and if it is a creative force, then it is scarcely extraordinary that the evolution of religious consciousness should show precisely the same characteristics which are found in biological evolution; namely, real creative novelty, real transformation, real irreducibility of the consequent to its antecedents, real difference between any given stage of development and the original one.

B. The Jungian View: Religious experience is an empirical type of experience, centered on psychological and organic affectivity, on the feelings and emotions, on what is submitted to passively.

For Jung, religion is an irreducible function inasmuch as it is "a spontaneous expression of a certain predominant psychological condition" (147). Religious experience therefore does not derive essentially from any objective content, which in fact varies endlessly, but from a subjective value-judgment. This judgment sees religious content as the symbol of the supreme value that the person concerned must aim at. Naturally, this kind of value-judgment takes the form of a personal experience.

Using Otto's concept, Jung would say that the numious is not posited, but imposes itself. Consciousness does not so much prompt it as submit to it. The numinous as such subjugates man independently of his will.

Both according to religious teaching and the general opinion of mankind, the activity of the numinous has its source in a region beyond the individual. Jung, as a scientist who has no wish to extrapolate his observations in the psychic field, does not feel justified in adopting this view, and so he gives this force a new name, the self, and vigorously excluding everything that lies outside the field of psychology, describes it as a psychic totality which, though it utterly transcends and overflows beyond the conscious ego, at the same time includes it and stands behind it as an impenetrable background (148). Hence he can define religion as "the attitude peculiar to a consciousness which has been altered by the experience of the numinosum," or in other words, the attitude of a consciousness that has submitted to the psychic totality insofar as this totality manifests itself as man's highest value.

Jung is agnostic with respect to the existence of a transcendent God. Epistemological criticism proves the impossibility of knowing God, but the psyche comes forward with the assertion of the experience of God. God is a psychic fact of immediate experience. This is a cornerstone for understanding Jung.

The whole idea of God is based on experience. Existence for Jung is synonymous with experience. Existence of God is therefore synonymous with experience of God. God is an object of personal experience. Depth psychology is concerned with the self-understanding of man, from the point of view not of knowledge, but of experience. The needful thing is not to "know" the truth but to experience it. Not to have an intellectual conception of things, but to find our way to the inner, perhaps wordless irrational experiences --- that is the heart of the problem according to Jung.

Kant's warning "not to venture with speculative reason beyond the limits of experience" has been highly honored by modern theologians. Some have thought to establish their theological concepts on the basis of a scientific or philosophical analysis of experience. Others have tried to show that theology is really a disguised anthropology.

Others, like Karl Barth, have been critical of the attempt to give human experience a significant role in the formation of theology. Yet even Barth witnesses to the influence of the Kantian dictum. He entirely agrees that speculative reason is bound to the limits of experience, and that is why there can be no valid natural theology, why our knowledge of God must be given in revelation. In another way, too, Barth illustrates the concern of modern theology with human experience. He insists that the knowledge given in revelation constitutes genuine human knowledge. Once received, it helps us to understand our human situation more fully and correctly than would be possible without it.

Bultmann, too, heeds Kant's warning. He regards it as settled that human reasoning cannot transcend the boundaries of experience, cannot find out God. Nor can we speak of God in rational, conceptual terms, for to do so would imply that He is an "object" within the spatio-temporal boundaries of experience. How, then, is theology possible? It is possible for one who sees that its intent is existential rather than speculative. We have no way of speaking conceptually about the God who encounters us, but we can speak of the impact of the encounter upon our understanding of self and our situation. The proper object of theology is, then, not God but the person.

Among others, Macquarrie maintains that the starting point of theology is man himself, and "faith can be seen as something that is rooted in the very constitution of our human existence." For him the purpose of theology is to "make sense" of existence, and his discussion of alternative ways of interpreting the human situation makes clear that, ideally, theology should make better sense than other formulations" (149).

Jung asserts that all the old ideas of God, indeed thought itself, and particularly numinous thought, have their origin in experience. Primitive man does not think his thoughts, they simply appear in his mind. Purposive and directed thinking is a relatively late human achievement. The numinous image is far more an expression of essentially unconscious processes than a product of rational inference. Consequently it falls into the category of psychological objects, and this raises the question of the underlying psychological assumptions.

Experience is an irrational datum not subject to human will and caprice. Experiences cannot be made. They happen --- yet fortunately their independence of the person's activity is not absolute but relative. We can draw closer to them --- that much lies within our human reach.

In Jung's view religious statements refer without exception to things that cannot be established as physical facts (150). If they did not do this, they would inevitably fall into the category of the natural sciences. Taken as referring to anything physical, they make no sense whatever, and science would dismiss them as non-experienceable.

The fact that religious statements frequently conflict with the observed physical phenomena proves that in contrast to physical perception the spirit is autonomous, and that psychic experience is to a certain extent independent of physical data. The psyche is an autonomous fact, and religious statements are psychic confessions which in the last resort are based on unconscious; i.e., on transcendental processes. These processes are not accessible to physical perception, but demonstrate their existence through the confessions of the psyche.

Every psychic process is an image and an "imagine." Otherwise no consciousness could exist and the occurrence would lack phenomenality. Imagination itself is a psychic process, for which reason it is completely irrelevant whether the enlightenment be called "real" or "imaginary." The person who has the enlightenment, or alleges that he has it, thinks at all events that he is enlightened. What others think about it decides nothing whatever for him in regard to his experience.

Jung strongly asserts that all religions contain logical contradictions and assertions that are impossible in principle (151). This is in fact the very essence of religious assertion. As witness to this we have Tertullian's avowal: "And the Son of God is dead, which is worthy of belief because it is absurd. And when buried He rose again, which is certain because it is impossible."

Jung says that, "If Christianity demands faith in such contradictions it does not seem to me that it can very well condemn those who assert a few paradoxes more." Oddly enough the paradox is one of our most valuable spiritual possessions, while uniformity of meaning is a sign of weakness. Hence a religion becomes inwardly impoverished when it loses or waters down its paradoxes; but their multiplication enriches because only the paradox comes anywhere near to comprehending the fullness of life. Non-ambiguity and non-contradiction are one-sided and thus unsuited to express the incomprehensible.

C. Religious Experience: Catholicism and Jung in dialogue.

There are several facets of Jung's explanation of experience that present problems to the Catholic. Jung tells us that "Religion means dependence on and submission to the irrational facts of experience. These do not refer directly to social and physical conditions; they concern far more the individual's psychic attributes" (152). Elsewhere Jung says that by the term "irrational" he is "not denoting something contrary to reason, but something beyond reason, something therefore, not grounded on reason" (153).

Apart from the dubious meaning Jung attaches to the word "irrational," there is a question about the passive position in which he regularly puts the person. Perhaps this passive position, in which the person is more acted upon than acting, explains a number of Jungian views. It would explain why, as Jung says,

> The unconscious is the only available source of religious experience. This is certainly not to say that what we call the unconscious is identical with God or is set up in His place. It is simply the medium from which religious experience seems to flow. As to what the further cause of such experience may be, the answer to this lies beyond the range of human knowledge. Knowledge of God is a transcendental problem (154).

The Catholic position is that much can be known about God through human reason. This position constitutes the rationale for natural theology. There is no doubt that every person subjects all incoming data to a psychic exposure that is personal and unique to the individual. This exposure does not rule out, though, the attainment of a common understanding by various people. If we were not able to lay aside our personal psychic disposition we would not be able to communicate with each other. And indeed, our institutions are full of people who are incapable of doing just that.

Jung asserts that

> Experience is an irrational datum not subject to human will and caprice. Experiences cannot be <u>made</u>. They happen --- yet fortunately their independence of man's activity is not absolute but relative. We can draw closer to them --- that much lies within our human reach. There are ways which bring us nearer to living experience, yet we should beware of calling these ways 'methods.' The way to experience, moreover, is anything but a clever trick; it is rather a venture which requires us to commit ourselves with our whole being (155).

There are at least two reactions that must be made to this statement. First, as Jung himself admits, the human mind has never yet rested content with experience alone. All mental development comes by way of speculation and not by confining ourselves to mere experience. Experience without speculation leads nowhere (156). And the mental processes whereby experience becomes meaningful must involve the rational. Second, much experience comes from outside the psychic dimension. Our window to the world is every bit as much our physical senses as it is our psychic sense. And as has been mentioned elsewhere, much of our psychic understanding is related to non-psychic symbols, such as the wheel and the door (157).

It may be helpful to call to mind again that the unconscious cannot be an object of any possible direct scientific inquiry. All statements about such a hypothetical subject matter depend on assumption drawn from certain types of conscious experience (158). With proper safeguards, Catholics can agree that the significance of the unconscious mind of the human race for religion can hardly be overestimated. The unconscious realm is a vast reservoir of new ideas. The implications which can be abstracted from the data of either the external or internal world seem a limitless capacity of the human mind. The unconscious side of personality contains much more than the unfulfilled ideas of which people are aware and to which they aspire. It contains countless ideas, plans, and possibilities as yet unthought of. Jung, of course, maintains that this inexhaustible capacity of the unconscious mind appears to be the basis for the infinite possibilities traditionally ascribed to God.

There is little question that the Catholic position sees common human experience as a principle source for theology (159). Jung carries his sense of experience beyond the Catholic one. As he regularly says, "The needful thing is not to 'know' the truth but to experience it. Not to have an intellectual conception of things, but to find our way to the inner, perhaps wordless, irrational experiences --- that is the heart of the problem" (160).

When we ask what kind of experience or what set of experiences contribute to the individuation process, Jung informs us that there is a wide configuration of experiences that either singularly or in tandem may direct us to our goal. The Jungian design worked out by Jolande Jacobi has striking similarities to the experiences that a person might have as he attempts to work out his religious expression (161). She lists the following as the various aspects of the individuation process:

1.   A) The "natural process which is the ordinary course of human life
        B) The "analytically assisted" process worked out by Jung.
2.   A) A process experienced and worked out as an "individual way"
        B) An initiation resulting from participation in a collective event
3.   A) A gradual development consisting of many little transformations
        B) A sudden transformation brought about by a shattering experience
4.   A) A continuous development extending over the whole life span
        B) A cyclic process constantly recurring in unchanged form
5.   A) A process in which only the first phases are accomplished
        B) A process in which the phases follow in sequence

6.   A) A process prematurely interrupted by out or inner circumstances
        B) An undeveloped process remaining in atrophied form
        C) A "sick" or "defective" process

According to Catholic teaching, our experience of God in this world involves three basic principles: 1) Our knowledge of God in this world is not an immediate, intuitive cognition, but a mediate, abstractive knowledge, because it is attained through the knowledge of creatures. 2) God's nature is incomprehensible to man. 3) Our knowledge of God is not proper but analogical.

While cognition properly so-called comprehends an object through its own mental form or by immediate vision, analogical cognition comprehends an object through an alien form. In the cognition of God in this world we apply concepts gained from created things to God on the ground of a certain similarity and ordination of the created things to Him as their efficient and exemplary cause. There is a relation of analogy between the creature and the Creator which is founded on the fact that the creature is necessarily made to the likeness of the Creator (162). This so-called analogy of being is sharply rejected by Karl Barth as the "invention of anti-Christ."

Despite this analogy or similarity, there is much greater dissimilarity between the creature and the Creator, namely the dissimilarity between the finite and the infinite. Our cognition of God in this world comes, as Pseudo-Dionysius the Areopagite taught, by the three-fold way of affirmation, negation and eminence.

Jung's empirical theory holds that man believes in God because he finds the basis for God in his own psychic nature. Jung does not speak of God as an idea, but when he speaks of God at all he means something quite different. God is not thought or contrived, nor is he apprehended and exhausted by our ideas. He is experienced.

As long as what a person experiences of God is alive, he is influenced by it. Jung associates the God-image with the power of imagination (163). Imagination is an actualization of the contents of the unconscious, which do not belong to the exterior world and are of an archetypal nature. The God-image that people make for themselves in idea is likewise a work of imagination --- that is to say, it is not so much a matter of knowledge of some fact external to the person as of the expression of a psychic fact, the best possible formulation of some psychic actuality which we have to exteriorize in order to grasp at all.

As to conclusions concerning the nature of God, two types emerge from psychological analysis. One type of conclusion describes the system of motivation and ideation which consciously or unconsciously provides the members of each particular religious group with the reality of their God. This type also describes how they conceptualize their God in natural or supernatural terms and how they adjust to him in their pattern of religious activities.

The other type of conclusion proceeds further by indicating from an empirical standpoint the particular reality in experience which most effectively performs the role of God and the way in which this reality is correctly conceptualized and appropriately influenced by the person. Although the system of religious reality responds when regarded in different ways, the quality of the response depends upon how the lines of reality are drawn, whether narrowly in terms of inaccessible ideals or broadly in terms of human love. The criterion of effectiveness as shown by the historical evolution of man's definition of God is what psychic constellation appears to be most productive of the highest benefits to the human race sought by participants in religion. The quality of the response made by the higher power also depends upon the extent to which our theological concepts referring to experience correctly represent what is present or latent in experience and upon the resulting adjustment which he makes to the higher power.

Jung's psychology is concerned with the self-understanding of the person, from the point of view not of knowledge, but of experience. Analytical psychology attempts to show how existence can be taken hold of, how the person is actuated, how the person can become authentic. Insofar, therefore, as this psychology serves the development of a personalistic view of the person, it is important for the realization of the life of faith, since it embraces us in our "depths" and makes it possible to summon the whole nature of the person and bring it into relation with Christianity. In the final chapter this realization will be more extensively examined.

In summary, the following points bear upon the discussion of religious experience. 1) Jungian religious experience is essentially individual. The person experiences God through the mechanism of his own soul and projects those experiences on to non-psychic phenomena. The Catholic religious experiences is essentially social. The person experiences God through non-psychic phenomena and relates such experiences to the workings of the soul. 2) The Jungian experience flows through the pardoxical and the irrational. For the Catholic, experience flows through the routine and the rational. It is this rational process that makes natural theology possible.

Jung maintains that his experience of God is direct, while that of Catholicism is indirect. Catholicism disputes Jung's contention. Finally, Jung relegates religious experience to the realm of the human alone, and he hypothesizes that nothing can be known about God outside the psychic processes. Catholicism on the other hand, states that God is an entity outside the psychic processes and is knowable as such.

Chapter IV

The relativity of "truth"
has been known for ages
and does not stand in the
way of anything, and if it
did would merely prevent
belief in dogmas and
authority. But it does
not even do that.

C.G. Jung
Freud and Psychoanalysis

SOUL AND PSYCHE

According to Jung, he does not presume to know what the theologian misunderstands or fails to understand in the empiricist's point of view, for "it is as much as I can do to learn to estimate his theological premises correctly" (164). If I am not mistaken, however, one of the main difficulties lies in the fact that both appear to speak the same language, but this language calls up in their minds two totally different fields of association. Both can apparently use the same concept and must then acknowledge, to their amazement, that they are speaking of two different things. Take, for instance, the word "God."

The theologian will naturally assume that the metaphysical Ens Absolutum is meant. The empiricist, on the contrary, does not dream of making such a far-reaching assumption, which strikes him as downright impossible anyway. He just as naturally means the word "God" as mere statement, or at most as an archetypal motif which prefigures such statements. For him "God" can just as well mean Yahweh, Allah, Zeus, Shiva, or Huitzilopochtli.

The question arises about the word "soul." Jung uses that word constantly in reference to psychic structure. Does it have the same meaning for Jung as is found in Catholic theology? It is to that question that we now turn.

I. The Third Presupposition: The Soul

A. <u>The Catholic View</u>: The human soul is the principle of the spiritual mental life, and at the same time, the principle of the corporeal (vegetative and sensitive) life.

There is a very complicated history to the idea of the "soul." In its biblical setting, soul means simply "the vitality of the flesh." The person becomes a soul and, upon death, becomes a "dead" soul. Ancient Christian thinkers were confronted with the Greek philosophical questions about the soul's immortality, pre-existence, and its possible emanation from the divine.

Irenaeus and others took up the Greek anthropological concerns and maintained that the soul was mortal. Origin held that the preexisting spirit is condemned to a worldly existence as a soul and that the person is doomed by nature to live by going out of himself --- an "ek-static" existence.

Gregory of Nyssa and Augustine continued to work from the Greek notion. For them the soul, in its spirit, participates in divine wisdom, which it exercises in contemplation. A turning point came with Aquinas. He went beyond the old distinction between matter and form to distinguish between being and essence. He saw in the very actualization of matter by spirit a resultant reality distinct from both, the human person (165).

In a very general way, the soul is understood to be the immaterial principle without which it seems impossible to explain the different movements and behavior of living beings in general, and the thought of human beings in particular (166). As a philosophical idea, the conception of the notion of soul took two different directions. One tended to emphasize the distance that separated soul from matter, and the other attempted to define as precisely as possible the soul's relationship to the matter it enlivened.

The first view insisted upon the immortality of the soul and on its essential difference between the body. This is, ultimately, the Platonic explanation. From Plato on, a whole philosophical tradition developed that was both intellectual and mystical, and of a profoundly dualistic inspiration. It held that the soul could reach the fullness of its destiny only through emptying itself through contemplation and reflection of the matter that holds it a prisoner.

The second tendency is not so much concerned with the essence of the soul, but rather with the way it gives life to living beings. Aristotle defines it as "that by which we live, feel, and especially think." (De Anima 414A, 12). It is that whereby life, which was a potency in the body, becomes act, namely, the form of the body.

The first view is identified with St. Augustine, the second with St. Thomas. It was not until Vatican II that the Magisterium broke out of the body-soul schema and began to implement the more contemporary approach. The key word is now person and not soul (167). The person is "one" in body and soul. In his "interiority" he transcends the totality of things. "Thus, when he recognizes in himself a spiritual and immortal soul, he is not being mocked by a deceptive fantasy. . . he is getting to the depths of the very truth of the matter." (Gaudium et Spes, art. 14).

Pope Pius XII in his address to the Fifth International Catholic Congress of Psychotherapy and Clinical Psychology held in Rome in 1953 suggested that psychologists and therapists ought to take account of this fact: the very existence of each faculty or psychological function has its warrant in the purpose of the whole. What makes a human being to be such is principally the soul, which is the essential form of his nature.

It is from this that flows, in the last analysis, the whole of human life; in it are rooted all psychological processes with their particular structures and organic laws; and it is to the soul that nature entrusts the government of all these energies to the extent that they have not yet attained their final determination. From this datum, which is at once ontological and psychological, it follows that it would be unrealistic to seek, whether in theory or in practice, to assign the function fo determining the whole to some particular factor --- for example, to one of the elementary psychic processes --- and thus to entrust the helm to a subordinate power. "It has been supposed that we should accentuate the opposition between metaphysics and psychology. This is quite wrong. The psychological realm itself still belongs to the realm of the ontological and the metaphysical" (168).

The commonly held Catholic view is that the supernatural presupposes and perfects nature (169). This means human nature in its entirety, in its bodily, even visceral depths, as well as in its spiritual and intellectual heights. For the thomist, the soul was one single life-principle, the very perfection, act, or form of the body, which produced both purely spiritual acts (and was therefore itself spiritual) and the functions of sensitive and vegetative life. It is not, as we know it in this world, a separate substance existing in its own right and having a life of its own; it is our life itself whereby we live. The manifestations of life, spiritual and corporeal,

103

conscious and unconscious, are activities of the numerous powers or abilities of this one actuality, which is the very actuality or form of the human body.

The soul, within the framework of a comprehensive notion of man, means the constitutive element by which human existence is capable, by nature, of attaining self-hood. If freedom, decision, responsibility and knowledge are essential determinations of man, so that he not merely has his freedom and consciousness but actually is these acts as he exercises them, then his nature, the principle of his acts, which goes beyond any actual exercise of them, must in himself make his basic activity possible. The soul is human nature in its self-awareness and the primary force of its subjectivity.

B. The Jungian View: The soul is a personification of the unconscious; it is a function of relation between the subject and the inaccessible depths of the unconscious.

For Jung the soul is a personification of the unconscious, where lies the treasure, the libido which is immersed in introversion and is allegorized as God's kingdom (170). This amounts to a permanent union with God, a living in His kingdom, in that state where a preponderance of libido lies in the unconscious and determines conscious life. The libido concentrated in the unconscious was formerly invested in objects, and this made the world seem all-powerful. God was then "outside," but now he works from within, as the hidden treasure conceived as God's kingdom.

If, then, Meister Eckhart reaches the conclusion that the soul is itself God's kingdom, it is conceived as a function of relation to God, and God would be the power working within the soul and perceived by it. Eckhart even calls the soul the image of God.

It is evident from the ethnological and historical material that the soul is a content that belongs partly to the subject and partly to the world of spirits; i.e., the unconscious. Hence the soul always has an earthly as well as a rather ghostly quality. But the soul never loses its intermediate position. It must therefore be regarded as a function of relation between the subject and the inaccessible depths of the unconscious. The determining force (God) operating from these depths is reflected by the soul; that is, it creates symbols and images, and is itself only an image. By means of these images the soul conveys the forces of the unconscious to consciousness; it is both receiver and transmitter, an organ for perceiving unconscious contents. What it perceives are symbols. But symbols are shaped energies, determining ideas whose affective power is just as great as their spiritual value.

The soul is our meeting place with God (171). And the soul is born in God when we become aware that our psyche is inseparable from God whose image is its center. So when we withdraw from the

105

world-introvert, in other words --- the libido that once flowed from us, outward, to the world and things now flows inward and activates the soul. God responds to this inner activation by drawing near and ultimately being born in us, that is, his presence is consciously recognized and acknowledged.

The human soul is neither a psychiatric nor a physiological, or a biological problem at all, but a psychological problem. The soul is a field of its own with its own laws. The nature of the soul cannot be derived from the principles of other fields of knowledge, otherwise the specific nature of the psychic is violated. It cannot be compared with the brain, nor with hormones, nor with any of the familiar instincts, but for good or ill it must be recognized as a phenomenon sui generis.

According to the Jungian, Josef Goldbrunner, the development and differentiation of the human soul was stimulated above all by the Enlightenment. But the various religions stood still and became torpid. Externally they had found an ideal and ritual form in which all the hopes and strivings of the soul are received and expressed. But the advancing differentiation of the soul soon outgrew the range of "the local religions of the West" and the existing forms of religion were no longer capable of embracing the whole fullness of spiritual life and the soul was left to its own devices. The Church no longer meets the soul with understanding. It speaks another tongue, it has different problems and different feelings.

The various religions, according to Goldbrunner, only give information about the mysteries of the soul; they are a symbolical expression of the process of individuation and lack all the qualities of a supernatural revelation. They lead man to the sources of life in his own soul --- unfortunately unconsciously. Prayer, the Sacraments, the following of the Commandments, meditation, Bible reading are all merely exercises toward the attainment of spiritual equilibrium, spiritual hygiene, mere psychology. All assertions about the other world, the world beyond, the Kingdom of God, grace and miracles, are projections of unconscious spiritual contents. All the relevant sayings of scripture and the symbols and institutions of Christianity can be explained "naturally."

In a symbolical form religions are an image of the collective unconscious. Jung tells us, "My attitude to all religions is therefore a positive one. In their teaching I recognize the figures which I have met in my patients' dreams and fantasies. In their morals I see the same or similar attempts which my patients make from their own invention or inspiration to find the right way to deal with the powers of the soul" (172).

The sacred rites, the ritual, the institutions and asceticism are extremely interesting as constantly changing and formally varied techniques of producing the right way. Man as a collective being "invented" the technique and passed on his experience from generation to generation. The various religions are therefore an expression of humanity's collective experience. Their language is symbolic. The symbol combines the two aspects of the sou, the unconscious and the conscious.

In the Catholic structure the soul is cojoined with the body. One is to be considered with the other. In the Jungian structure the soul is considered with the psyche. One does not make sense without the other. Jung states that he has been compelled, in his investigations into the structure of the unconscious, to make a conceptual distinction between soul and psyche. By psyche Jung understands the totality of all psychic processes, conscious as well as unconscious (173). By soul, on the other hand, he understands a clearly demarcated functional complex that can best be described as a "personality." The psyche, then, is the total inner world; the soul is a major component of that inner world since it is the maker of images and the keeper of symbols.

The psyche is the only phenomenon that is given to us immediately and therefore, is the *sine qua non* of all experience (174). The only things we experience immediately are the contents of consciousness. In saying this Jung claims that he is not attempting to reduce the "world" to his "idea" of it.

Going further, Jung maintains that every science is a function of the psyche, and all knowledge is rooted in it. The psyche is the greatest of all cosmic wonders and the way to understanding the world as an object. It is in the highest degree odd that Western man, with few exceptions, apparently pays so little regard to this fact. Swamped by the knowledge of external objects, the subject of all knowledge has been temporarily eclipsed to the point of seeming non-existence.

It does not surprise Jung that psychology debouches into philosophy, for the thinking that underlies philosophy is after all a psychic activity which, as such, is the proper study of psychology (175). "I always think of psychology as encompassing the whole of the psyche, and that includes philosophy and theology and many other things besides. For underlying all philosophies and all religions are the facts of the human soul, which may ultimately be the arbiters of truth and error" (176).

Jung believes that the moral order, the idea of God, religion itself, have not dropped into man's lap from outside, straight down from heaven, as it were, but that man contains all this in nuce within himself, and for this reason can produce it all out of himself. The ideas of the moral order and of God belong to the ieradicable substrate of the human soul (177).

Jung says that in physics we can do without a God-image, but in psychology it is a definite fact that has got to be reckoned with, just as have to reckon with "affect," "instinct," and "mother." It is the fault of the everlasting contamination of object and imago that people can make no conceptual distinction between "God" and

"God-image" one is speaking of God and offering "theological" explanations (178).

It is not for psychology, as a science, to demand a hypostatization of the God-image. But, the facts being what they are, it does have to reckon with the existence of a God-image. In the same way it reckons with instinct but does not deem itself competent to say what "instinct" really is. The psychological factor is in itself. It is equally clear that the God-image corresponds to a definite complex of psychological facts, and is thus a quantity which we can operate with; but what God is in himself remains a question outside the competence of all psychology.

What appears to us as immediate reality consists of carefully processed images, and, furthermore, we live immediately only in a world of images. In order to determine, even approximately, the real nature of material things we need the elaborate apparatus and complicated procedures ofo chemistry and physics. These disciplines are really tools which help the human intellect to cast a glance behind the deceptive veil of images into a non-psychic world.

Far, therefore, from being a material world, this is a psychic world, which allows us to make only indirect and hypothetical inferences about the real nature of matter. The psychic alone has immediate reality, and this includes all forms of the psychic, even "unreal" ideas and thoughts which refer to nothing "external." We may call them "imagination" or "delusion," but that does not detract in any way from their effectiveness. Indeed, there is no "real" thought that cannot, at times, be thrust aside by an "unreal" one, thus proving that the latter is stronger and more effective than the former.

Greater than all physical dangers are the tremendous effects of delusional ideas, which are yet denied all reality by our world-blinded consciousness. Our much vaunted reason and our boundlessly overestimated will are sometimes utterly powerless in the face of "unreal" thoughts. The world-powers that rule over all mankind, for good or ill, are unconscious psychic factors, and it is they that bring consciousness into being and hence create the *sine qua non* for the existence of any world at all. We are steeped in a world that was created by our own psyche.

Psychological truth by no means excludes metaphysical truth, though psychology, as a science, has to hold aloof from all metaphysical assertions. Its subject is the psyche and its contents. Both are realities, because they work (179). Though we do not possess a physics of the soul, and are not even able to observe it and judge it from some Archimedean point "outside" ourselves, and can therefore know nothing objective about it since all knowledge of the psyche (180) is itself psychic; in spite of all this the soul is the only expedient of life and existence. It is, in fact, the only immediate experience we can have. The symbols it creates are always grounded in the unconscious archetype, but their manifest forms are molded by the ideas acquired by the conscious mind.

C. The Soul: Catholicism and Jung in dialogue.

Pius X in his condemnation of modernism states that there are three errors in which faith is said to be subject to science (181).

> The first: that in any religious fact, after the divine reality has been taken away, and whatever experience he who believes has of it, all others things, especially religious formulae, do not pass beyond the confines of phenomena, and so fall under science. Second: although it is said that God is the object of faith alone, this is to be granted with regard to the divine reality, but not with regard to the idea of God. For this is subject to science which, while it philosophizes in the logical order, as they say, attains also what is absolute and ideal. Therefore, philosophy or science has the right to learn about the idea of God, and to direct it in its evolution, and, if anything extraneous enters it, to correct it. Finally it happens that God does not suffer duality within Himself, and so the believer is urged on by an innermost force so to harmonize faith with science that it never disagrees with the general idea which science sets forth about the entire universe. Thus, then, is it effected that science is entirely freed from faith, that faith on the other hand, however much it is proclaimed to be extraneous to science, is subject to it.

> Pius moves from the philosopher to the modernist theologian (182). In theology, the Pontiff states, the modernist makes use of the same principles that we saw employed by the philosopher, and he adapts them to the believer; we mean the principles of immanence and

112

symbolism. It is held as certain by the philosopher that the principle of faith is immanent; it is added by the believer that this principle is God; and he himself (the theologian) concludes: God, then, is immanent in man. From this comes theological immanence. Again, to the philosopher it is certain that the representations of the object of faith are only symbolical; to the believer, likewise, it is certain that the object of faith is God in Himself; so the theologian gathers that the representations of the divine reality are symbolical. From this comes theological symbolism.

As we noted earlier, Jung is subject to these charges because, from a magisterial point of view, he is promoting a psychological modernism. There are some few signs that the controversial elements of modernism are receiving a renewed scrutiny by theologians. Perhaps at some future time the ultimate historical assessment of Jung's modernistic tendencies will be tempered.

Perhaps Jung himself best summarizes his defense:

There is no question of my producing incontrovertible truths --- they are simply ideas thrown out in an attempt to bring a bit of order into the bewildering conglomeration of psychic realities . . . all our present psychological theories are subjective assertions which we defend jealously, in a highly partisan spirit, because they echo powerful currents in the human soul. When we have amassed something like all these assertions we shall be able at some future date to compare them together and so reach a deeper understanding of the nature of the soul. In the meantime the founder of any psychological theory must try to reconcile himself to the fact that he will be not only a founder but a martyr as well (183).

It is certainly not within the professional competence of the empirical psychologist to judge the truth of the relative claims made by Yahweh, Allah, Zeus, and the rest. But he can hardly fail to note that, even as phenomena, they are by no means identical, and fidelity to his very empiricism demands that he should observe their differences no less than their seemingly common characteristics. The psychological fact is that to their respective devotees it is the differences rather than the similarities which are of paramount importance.

The denial of the right to the name "religious" to the imageless and emotionless "Dark Night" of St. John of the Cross, or to the consciously and rationally argued Deus Est of St. Thomas Aquinas, or the devaluation of their procedures as secondary variations or accidental deviations from the essential religious past, would argue an arbitrary a priorism which is the negation of objective empiricism. The plea, then, to psychologists in general, and to Jungians in particular, is not for any departure from empirical methods, but rather for their more rigorous and comprehensive application.

Jung maintains that when he points out that the soul possess by nature a religious function and when he stipulates that it is the prime task of all education (of adults) to convey the archetype of the God-image, or its emanations and affects, to the conscious mind, then it is precisely the theologian who seizes him by the arm

114

and accuses him of "psychologism." Jung asserts that he did not attribute a religious function to the soul, but rather he merely produced the facts which prove that the soul is <u>naturaliter religiosa</u>; i.e., possesses a religious function. He did not invent or insinuate this function; it produces itself of its own accord without being prompted there by any opinions or suggestions of his (184).

In <u>Psychology and Alchemy</u>, Jung writes,

> With a truly tragic delusion some theologians fail to see that it is not a matter of proving the existence of the light, but of blind people who do not know that their eyes could see. It is high time we realized that is pointless to praise the light and preach it if nobody can see it. It is much more needful to teach people the art of seeing. For it is obvious that far too many people are incapable of establishing a connection between the sacred figures and their own psyche; they cannot see to what extent the equivalent images are lying dormant in their own unconscious. In order to facilitate this inner vision we must first clear the way for the faculty of seeing. How this is to be done without psychology, that is, without making contact with the psyche, is frankly beyond my comprehension (185).

Goldbrunner, writing from the Catholic position, maintains that there is a weakness in Jung's therapy. He came to this conclusion through his work with suffering clients. The human psyche is more than a spiritual organism, the powers of which can be brought into harmony under the medical eye of the therapist. It is true that many people are content with the partial well-being which they call "health" but spirituality they have been beheaded. The human psyche is a spiritual being which points by its very nature beyond the psychic realm to the metaphysical world. Goldbrunner asserts that this whole dimension is leveled down by Jung and reduced to the intra-psychic sphere inasmuch as he interprets problems of truth as problems of psychological necessity. A whole province of the psyche, its supreme province, the "eye of the soul," namely the intellect, is dimmed and turned inwards with the information that nothing can be known outside the psychic sphere and that the "thing in itself," is hidden.

For Goldbrunner, this information fences in the eye of the soul; it dare not peep through the holes out of respect for such enlightened knowledge and it resigns itself to the inner vision of psychic images of all the objects which it "naively" presumes are on the other side of the fence. All healing is expected to come from the process of spiritual growth, from the contact between consciousness and the unconscious, from the development of spiritual individuality in the self.

Therefore Jung's patients are led to revere the psyche and confide in its nature but they receive no guidance from objective truths, objective values and the demands they make. The ego is called on to serve the growth of the soul but it is not confronted with the necessity of deciding on matters of truth. The world of metaphysics is exchanged for the world of the soul instead of their both being united.

According to Goldbrunner, Jung teaches his patients how to feel at home in the house of the soul but he locks them up in it; the door to transcendence is barred (186). But the human spirit realizes itself not merely in the process of growth, but also in making decisions since it is a personal spirit. If it is to attain its full development, it must have demands made upon it and that can happen not only as a result of numinous experience, by the extension of consciousness and contact with the original foundations of the unconscious, all of which are necessary first steps, but rather by a call from the transcendent and by an answer given with a full sense of responsibility and self-commitment. In such decisions the person acts and comes to freedom.

Modern psychology has one thing in common with modern physics, that its method enjoy greater intellectual recognition than its subject. Its subject, the psyche, is so infinitely diverse in its manifestations, so indefinite, and so unbounded, that the definitions given of it are difficult if not impossible to interpret. The following example demonstrates the problem.

"Soul" is the English of Latin anima, and anima is the Latin of Greek psyche. We cannot of course argue conclusively to an identity of subject-matter from the fact that psychologists use the same word, psyche, for their own field of investigation, but quite certainly they cannot legitimately claim that their field is something distinct from that covered by the traditional anima, psyche or soul.

The British Catholic psychitatrist, E.B. Strauss, suggests that it is important to assert from the start that the psyche with which the medical psychologists deal is conceptually different from the soul as defined by the theologian. By the psyche we mean the sum total of what we experience both <u>actually</u> and <u>potentially</u> --- actual experience constituting the conscious, latent and potential experience the unconscious.

It must be noted that Aquinas would be a most unsuitable patron saint for the view that the psychic apparatus is not the soul and the soul is not the psyche (187). 'Soul" is the English of the Latin 'anima;' and for Aquinas anima is the Latin of the Greek 'psyche.' For Aquinas, as for the magisterium, this 'soul' means the principle of life which differentiates living matter from dead matter; it is the source of everything in the individual which is alive. Whenever there is any manifestations of life, voluntary or involuntary, conscious or unconscious, there is a manifestation of soul.

The soul of theology is conceived of in terms of a different kind of discipline. The soul is that part of a person which is unique, individually created, endowed with survival value. It perceives true and real values, not only phenomena, and is modified by values. The soul is a theological concept, and hence only understandable in theological and ontological terms, whereas the psyche is a psychological construct.

Victor White points out a serious problem even if we discount the formal distinction of soul and psyche and maintain a distinction of the supernatural life of grace in the soul from its purely natural activities (188). If we maintain the Catholic principle "grace perfects nature," should we not expect an exact correspondence between an individual's holiness and his health, his sanctity and his sanity? Should we not even expect all devout believers to be sane and, from the psychologist's standpoint, fully mature and balanced individuals, and believers to be neurotic and unbalanced in proportion to their unbelief? The fact that this is apparently not so is the commonest and perhaps the most weighty of the objections brought forward against a positive correlation of religion and psychology.

If they do not share virtually the same perception of "soul," Jung and Catholicism are in agreement that the soul deals with our understanding, memory, imagination, inner senses, feelings, and drives. They both maintain that by penetrating into the soul, we are penetrating into the central mystery of our own being. For both, the soul bespeaks an individual possessing a spiritual nature.

The soul, then, becomes the doorway to the whole of reality. Catholic teaching has always maintained that the soul compels the person to seek unlimited knowledge and unlimited good. The fact no infinite goal can satisfy that craving prompts the positing of an infinite reality perceptible by natural theology. The human spirit is made to know and to love finite objects, but the dynamism which animates this knowledge and this love carries both of them irresistibly, even unconsciously, beyond any finite object.

There is an at least latent sense of the Catholic position in the now famous words penned by Jung in 1932:

> During the past thirty years people from all the civilized countries of the earth have consulted me. . . Among all my patients in the second half of life --- that is to say, over thirty-five --- there has not been one whose problem in the last resort was not that of finding a religious outlook on life. It is safe to say that every one of them fell ill because he had lost that which the living religions of every age have given to their followers, and none of them has been really healed who did not regain this religious outlook (189).

The healed, according to Jung, have found the soul for which they searched. This soul, for Jung and for Catholicism, is the meeting place where we experience the presence of God. As Jung tells us,

> It would be blasphemy to assert that God can manifest Himself everywhere save only in the human soul. Indeed the very intimacy of the relationship between God and the soul automatically precludes any devaluation of the latter. It would be going perhaps too far to speak of an affinity; but at all events the soul must contain in itself the faculty of relation to God, i.e., a correspondence, otherwise a connection could never come about. This correspondence is, in psychological terms, the archetype of the God-image (190).

Jung tells us that

> If the human soul is anything, it must be of unimaginable complexity and diversity. I can only gaze with wonder and awe at the depths and heights of our psychic nature. Its non-spatial universe conceals in untold abundance of images which have accumulated over millions of years of living development and become fixed in the organism. My consciousness is like an eye that penetrates to the most distant spaces, yet it is the psychic non-ego that fills them with non-spatial images. And these images are not pale shadows, but tremendously powerful psychic factors. ...Besides this picture I would like to place the spectacle of the starry heavens at night, for the only equivalent of the universe within is the universe without; and just as I reach this world through the medium of the body, so I reach that world through the medium of the psyche (191).

We can close this chapter, keeping in mind the following points. 1) Here, perhaps more than anything else, the Catholic and the Jungian view merge. The "soul" of Catholicism and the "psyche" of Jung are related, though not identical, terms. 2) Both Catholicism and Jung are agreed that the soul is a naturally religious faculty. 3) For Catholicism, the soul is the major spiritual principle of the human person. For Jung the soul is the major part of the major principle of the human person, namely, the psyche. 4) For Catholicism, the soul is the reflection of the God who made it, yet that maker lies outside the soul's boundaries. For Jung, the soul is the reflection of the God who resides there in some psychic form.

Chapter V

Levi-Strauss: "The ultimate
aim of the human sciences is
not to construct man but to
dissolve him."

From Fierro's The Militant Gospel

THE STRUCTURE AND BEHAVIOR OF THE HUMAN PERSON

A. The Jungian View

Every theological and every psychological point of view must be measured by its ability to find acceptance among the very people whom it purports to define or to describe. The ultimate strength of any system is acceptance, an acceptance that helps people interpret their past, make sense of the present, and plan for the future. In this chapter we see what it is that both the Jungian and the Catholic systems ask us to accept as we reflect upon who we are and what we do.

Does a religious factor exist in the person? For Jung the existence of a religious factor in us is not an a priori principle. It is rather an empirical conclusion derived from the examination of countless numbers of patients who came to him for help. The manifestations of the religious function are so extraordinary and unusual, and its properties are so different from those of other human functions, that there is no possibility of reducing religion to any other human activity. The spiritual, Jung says, appears in the psyche as a drive, indeed a true passion. It is not derivative from another drive but a principle *sui generis*, namely the indispensable primitive power in the world of drives.

Why are religions invested with therapeutic power? Because religion is an important factor in human personality and, consequently, its absence produces natural psychic disturbances. The conscious mind may ignore its presence, but the factors are there, in the unconscious, and the more the ego tries to repress them, the greater the disturbances, and the greater the autonomy and power of the complexes of the collective unconscious. Religion is, in this sense, a form of psychic therapy, and one of the greatest helps in the psychological process of adaptation.

Certainly for the believer the Christian religion is not a psychotherapy if we understand by this term a method for establishing psychic balance without recourse to a transcendent principle. But every religion comprehends a psychotherapy to the extent that it reconciles the person with the psychic and cosmic forces which weigh upon his destiny (192).

Not only is it "high treason" from the theologian's point of view to say you believe in God because it is helpful to believe in Him --- it may even be wondered whether, therapeutically, this type of attitude applied to any aspect of religious life is as helpful as Jung thinks (193). As another writer has suggested, "We are faced by paradox: religion can be therapeutic only when it is not so regarded; when, instead, it is paid allegiance as a thing-in-itself" (194).

"The world was created imperfect, and God has placed man in it that he may perfect it" (195). So said Paracelsus. The Jungian psychotherapist considers the perfection of man's inner image as the primary task confronting man as he sets about to perfect the world. And it is the psychotherapeutic techniques of Carl Jung that provide the modus operandi by which man can perfect his inner image (196). Jung is insistent that his psychotherapy is congruent with modern man's search for spiritual values. He chides the analysts who are followers of Freud and Adler because both of them are "hostile to spiritual values" (197).

William Johnson writes that Jung's system is a "practical science" rather than an academic one (198). To investigate the psyche as the organ with which we are endowed for comprehending the existing universe, to observe its phenomena, to describe them, and to bring them into a meaningful system are his aims and goals. Jolande Jacobi writes, "The theological, psychological, historical, physical and biological standpoints as well as many others are all equally starting points for the investigation of the facts of being; they are inter-changeable, even transposable up to a certain point, and they can be utilized at will according to the investigator's problems and special interests (199). Jung takes the psychological, leaving the others to persons competent in their fields, drawing however upon his wide acquaintance with psychic reality, so that his theoretical structure is no abstract system created by the speculative intellect but an erection upon the solid ground of experience and resting only upon that.

Jung's analytical psychology must be conceived of in terms of its objective of healing or salvation (200). It intends to do so in a practical way, encouraging the individual to find the means of his own healing. Wholeness of personality is attained when the two parts of the psyche, the conscious and the unconscious, are joined together and stand in a living relation to one another.

Psychic wholeness is always a relative notion, a realization of man's being which is an objective to be grasped during the entire life of man (201). "The personality as a full realization of the wholeness of our being is an unattainable ideal. Unattainability is, however, never anything against an idea; for ideals are nothing but signposts, never goals" (202). The full realization of personality can never become an historical actuality because the unconscious contains the greater amount of energy.

Jung's impossible ideal brings with it the potentialities for the person to become truly human. It means that the person stands aloof from the undifferentiatedness and unconscious of the "herd;" it means that the person accepts the call of destiny found deep within his own unconscious (203).

"Only he who deliberately says 'yes' to the power of the destiny within himself becomes a personality" (204). Only then does he possess the ability to become part of a community, "to be an integral part of a group of human beings and not merely a cipher in the mass, which always consists only of a sum of people and never can become, like the community, a living organism that receives life and bestows life" (205).

Jung is the modern psychologist who has restored the religious factor in the person, thus setting up the long awaited bridge between psychology and religion. We have maintained throughout this work that Jung's ideas of religion and God cannot be properly understood and appreciated without an analysis of his presuppositions.

It is necessary to look more carefully at the personality structure that Jung theorizes is at the heart of our understanding of the human person. The Catholic magisterial view, works from a construct of body and soul, intellect and will. The Jungian perception is in sharp contrast to some of those traditional usages. The perceptions that Jung employs mold the presuppositions which he holds. The components of these perceptions include Jung's view of energy, fantasy, symbol and archetype.

We cannot understand Jung's concept of analytical psychology without averting to the principle of opposites. According to Jung, the root of psychological drives lies in a double polarity which constitutes the quintessence of life. Energy is crucial to Jung's system and there is no energy without the tension of the opposites.

For Jung, the opposites are the key to the dynamics of human personality. If polarity and opposition are universal laws, then, nothing can exist without its opposite and, therefore, every psychological extreme secretly contains its own opposite or stands in some sort of intimate and essential relation to it. As a consequence of this polarity everything in nature is found in natural pairs, a prerequisite for polarity and opposition. For instance, there is good and evil, masculine and feminine, death and life, conscious and unconscious, anima and animus, persona and shadow, and so forth.

The opposites are compensatory of each other, that is to say, one opposite compensates the deficiencies of the other opposite, thus balancing the complex elements of human personality. The compensatory function of the opposites is an expression of the self-defense mechanism; for example, extraversion compensates introversion, the unconscious compensates the conscious mind, the ego compensates the anima, and vice versa. Compensation also exists in the realm of ethics where evil compensates the good and vice versa. The compensatory function of the opposites is automatic, free from the arbitrary control of our will.

Opposition and duality play an important role in the development of human personality. Duality is not a luxury but a prerequisite of growth, and needs to be preserved by all means. In the last stage of the process of development, however, duality and opposition are harmonized and integrated into a higher synthesis. It is unity and wholeness, says Jung, the goal of man, which is symbolically expressed by the most important archetype of man, the archetype of the self. The process of man toward his goal, namely, wholeness which is intimately connected with religious content, is called by Jung the process of individuation (206).

Jung's most fundamental hypothesis is undoubtedly that of the libido or psychic energy. As an undifferentiated force manifesting itself in all psychic process, it lies at the root of an instinctual substrate common to all men and women. Jung says that the libido with which we operate is not only not concrete or known, but is a complete X, a pure hypothesis, a model or counter, and is no more concretely conceivable than the energy known to the world physics. Libido is intended simply as a name for the energy which manifests itself in the life-process and is perceived subjectively as conation and desire.

Libido can never be apprehended except in a definite form; that is to say, it is identical with fantasy-images. And we can only release it from the grip of the unconscious by bringing up the corresponding fantasy-images. However little Jung himself at first may have realized it, his concept of the libido meant at the very outset that psychology and religion could no longer follow their several paths without some merging. Indeed, it is clear from the opening chapters of The Psychology of the Unconscious that Jung was led to this conception of the undifferentiated energy by the fact that he was constantly presented by his patients with symbols which comparative religion showed to be universal symbols among mankind for the creative and undifferentiated Divinity.

Jung himself saw this clearly, but he seems to have been content to regard God as a fantasy concretization of his libido instead of drawing the conclusion that his libido is actually realized only in God, or that in its manifold manifestations it indicates an innate aspiration --- a natural desire for God. In positing an undifferentiated libido Jung was, in spite of himself, asserting that the psychological data were unaccountable except as a postulate which was as metaphysical as could be. For traditional metaphysics formless energy is synonymous with pure act, and pure act (under the name of libido) is, as natural theologians have pointed out, what we call God.

It is nearly impossible to exaggerate the importance that fantasy has for Jung's psychology. He tells us in Psychological Types that the psyche creates reality every day (207). The only expression to use for this activity is fantasy. Fantasy is just as much feeling as thinking; as much intuition as sensation. There is no psychic function that, through fantasy, is not inextricably bound up with the other psychic functions. Sometimes it appears in primordial form, sometimes it is the ultimate and boldest product of all our faculties combined.

Fantasy, therefore, seems to Jung to be the clearest expression of the specific activity of the psyche. It is pre-eminently, the creative activity from which the answers to all answerable questions come; it is the mother of all possibilities where, like all psychological opposites, the inner and outer worlds are joined together in living union. Fantasy it was and ever is which fashions the bridge between the irreconcilable claims of subject and object, introversion and extroversion. In fantasy alone both mechanisms are united.

Again, in The Practice of Psychotherapy, Jung remarks that when all is said and done, we can never rise above fantasy. It is true that there are unprofitable, futile, morbid and unsatisfying fantasies whose sterile nature is immediately recognized by every person endowed with common sense; but the faulty performance proves nothing against the normal performance. All the works of men and women have their origin in creative imagination. Jung asks, what right, then, have we to disparage fantasy? In the normal course of things, fantasy does not easily go astray; it is too deep for that, and too closely bound up with the tap-root of human and animal instinct. It has a surprising way of always coming out right in the end (208).

For Jung, there are two kinds of thinking; directed thinking and fantasy-thinking. The former operates with speech elements for the purpose of communication, and is difficult and exhausting; the latter is effortless, working as it were spontaneously, with the contents ready to hand, and guided by unconscious motives. The one produces innovations and adaptation, copies reality, and tries to act upon it; the other turns away from reality, sets free subjective tendencies, and, as regards adaptation, is unproductive.

We now know that the archaic thinking previously attributed only to children and primitives occupies a large place in the life of modern man and appears as soon as directed thinking ceases. Any lessening of interest, or the slightest fatigue, is enough to put an end to the delicate psychological adaptation to reality which is expressed through directed thinking, and to replace it by fantasies. We wander from the subject and let our thoughts go their own way;

if the slackening of attention continues, we gradually lose all sense of the present, and fantasy gains the upper hand.

It is in creative fantasies that we find the unifying function we seek. All the functions that are active in the psyche converge in fantasy (209). Fantasy has, it is true, a poor reputation among psychologists, and up to the present psychoanalytic theories have treated it accordingly. For Freud as for Adler, it is nothing but a "symbolic" disguise for the basic drives and intentions presupposed by these two investigators. As against these opinions it must be emphasized --- not on theoretical grounds but essentially for practical reasons --- that although fantasy can be causally explained and devalued in this way, it nevertheless remains the creative matrix of everything that has made progress possible for humanity. Fantasy has its own irreducible value, for it is a psychic function that has its roots in the conscious and the unconscious alike, in the individual as much as in the collective.

Continual conscious realization of unconscious fantasies, together with active participation in the fantasies, has the effect firstly of extending the conscious horizon by the inclusion of numerous unconscious contents; secondly of gradually diminishing the dominant influence of the unconscious; and thirdly of bringing about a change of personality.

Another dimension important to understanding the Jungian person resides in the human production of symbols. According to Jung,

132

when the psychologist takes an interest in symbols, he is primarily concerned with "natural" symbols as distinct from "cultural" symbols (210). The former are derived from the unconscious contents of the psyche, and they therefore represent an enormous number of variations on the basic archetypal motifs. In many cases, they can be traced back to their archaic roots, i.e., to ideas and images that we meet in the most ancient records and in primitive societies.

"Cultural" symbols, on the other hand, are those that have expressed "eternal truths" or are still in use in many religions. They have gone through many transformations and even a process of more of less conscious elaboration, and in this way have become the collective representations of civilized societies. Nevertheless, they have retained much of their original numinosity, and they function as positive or negative "prejudices" with which the psychologist has to reckon very seriously.

Symbols are never thought out consciously; they are always produced from the unconscious in the way of so-called revelation, or intuition. The symbol's richness of meaning leads to its lack of clarity. Since it includes the unconscious and looks toward the future it cannot possibly be fully exhausted by conscious analysis. There is therefore only one suitable attitude to be adopted towards it, that of receptive waiting, so as to enter bit by bit into its full meaning though it impresses itself upon us at once by its mysterious power of attraction.

Jung maintains that the reductive method, which interprets every symbolic expression as a mere sign of something sexul, misses the true significance of the symbol. He therefore sets up against it --- as a complementary method, not one to take its place, as he himself says in so many words --- the synthetic or constructive method. This starts by regarding the products of the unconscious as symbolic expressions that show in advance what possibilities there are of any future psychic development. It is therefore not so much a case of discovering real past attitudes towards people and things as of finding out the present subjective attitude towards them. As this is only expressed unconsciously in symbols, their meaning has to be gradually disentangled so as to help towards a new orientation of consciousness in harmony with the unconscious predispositions.

The image is closely attached to the symbol. It is the concentrated expression of the psychic situation as a totality activated by an object. This activated totality or constellation is the result of the activity of the unconscious as well as the conscious attitude. It is objective because it is nourished by the object, though not identical with sense-perception of it; subjective, because at the same time it expresses the subject's reaction, with all the unconscious elements totalized or constellated around the perception.

134

The double function of images is to contribute to consciousness something of the richness of the contents of the unconscious and, at the same time, to protect consciousness against being overwhelmed by the unconscious. The subject of concern for both this attraction and defense is the sanity of one's psychic life, the health of the individual as a whole.

Insofar as symbolic systems pass through historical stages, such images may go from a primitive order of objectification, through a fruitful elaborate system, to an otiose, jejune state in which the images of the system have lost their affective power. In the last condition, the individual is no longer protected against the "perils to his soul" by the socially available systems of symbols. For example, when the religion in which he was raised ceases to function significantly for his psychic life, he is confronted with the necessity of "re-making" himself.

Jung's explanation of the psychic structure ultimately hinges on the archetype. Along with the instinct, the archetype makes up the contents of the collective unconscious. The great power of the archetype comes directly from the role that it plays in the scheme of nature (211). The patterns of behavior of each species contain their characteristic proto-images inherent in their nature, and these supply the meaningful direction of the organism's life. It is the proto-image that eventually becomes the archetype, for it provides the underlying psychic patterns and directs the individual's activities from a level far below consciousness.

Just as the proto-images function to provide the essential purpose and drive behind animal patterns of behavior, so the archetypes fulfill the equivalent function in the person. They are not the instincts themselves, but they guide the instincts. They give the instincts their direction. They give them form. They outline the stages and phases through which the instincts must pass in human life.

The archetypes are very close to the instincts, and neither is able to function without the other; but they are the opposite poles of the process by which the individuality of the person is eventually achieved. The archetypes are the psychic devices that nature has provided for taking human instincts in the direction in which they are intended --- in which they are equipped, and indeed, in which they need to go.

Jung tells us that instincts are not vague and indefinite by nature, but are specifically formed motive forces which, long before there is any consciousness, and in spite of any degree of consciousness later on, pursue their inherent goals. Consequently, they form very close analogies to the archetypes, so close, in fact that there is good reason for supposing that the archetypes are the unconscious images of the instincts themselves, in other words, that they are patterns of instinctual behavior.

The normal process of individuation leads through the archetypal situation. Jung's psychology teaches us how to take this path consciously. The task is always the same: the struggle with the uncanny power from the depth. The Indian yogi must resist the enticements and threats of the deities and demons; the saint resists the devil and his paramours, and modern man strives to free himself from the "embrace of the unconscious."

With Jung the technique of differentiating the ego from the collective unconscious comes into its own. But the ego must always defend itself against a dual danger. One is the identification with evil which results in an uncanny influence on consciousness (212). The second danger to which one almost always succumbs to some extent is "that one admires oneself a little for having looked more deeply than others" (213).

The individuation process, as the way of development and maturation of the psyche, does not follow a straight line, nor does it always lead onwards and upwards (214). The course it follows is rather "stadial," consisting of progress and regress, flux and stagnation in alternating sequence. Only when we glance back over a long stretch of the way can we notice the development. If we wish to mark out the way somehow or other, it can equally well be considered a "spiral," the same problems and motifs occurring again and again on different levels. Eric Neumann described the individuation process as an interior Odyssey which he called "centroversion" (215). Jung spoke of it as a "labyrinthine" path, and said of it that the longest way is at the same time the shortest.

There are various possibilities in the individuation process:

1.   A) The "natural process" which is the ordinary course of human life.
      B) The "methodically" or "analytically assisted" process worked out by Jung.
2.   A) A process experienced and worked out as an "individual way"
      B) An initiation resulting from participation in a collective event.
3.   A) A gradual development consisting of many little transformations
      B) A sudden transformation brought about by a shattering experience
4.   A) A continuous development extending over the whole life span
      B) A cyclic process constantly recurring in unchanged form.

The aim of the individuation process is a synthesis of all partial aspects of the conscious and the unconscious psyche. It seems to point to an ultimately unknowable, transcendent "center" of the personality which, paradoxically, is at the same time its periphery, and is of the "highest intensity," possessing an extraordinary power of irradiation. This center and periphery Jung calls the Self, and he terms it the origin and fulfillment of the ego.

The process of individuation, at least for the individual, ends with the Self, an ultimate state never completely attained. The cycle from the undifferentiated collective unconscious through the

138

persona and the anima is completed with the Self. But for Jung that is not the last word. Each individuation enriches in its turn the culture and the collective unconscious, comparable to the stages through which the individual must pass. Cosmic history, like the history of the individual, is therefore the result of a spirit moving the whole universe by a process of differentiation and reintegration repeated on a number of levels.

The Self represents the first reality of human life, for it contains the primary constituents of what comprises specifically human nature. At the same time, the Self represents the culminating phase that brings the process of psychological integration to completion. This is really the same fact seen from another angle, for the fulfillment of the Self as a proto-image is necessarily the end result of the process as a whole. The Self is thus both beginning and end of human life. It is the primal psychoid potentiality from which human development comes. It is the goal that draws this development forward and it is the ultimate achievement when the goal is reached.

Between the Self as the beginning and the Self as the end result of human development there lies the process of individuation. The process is difficult to define, not only because it contains certain inherent obscurities as a psychological conception, but because, if we could define "individuation" with precision, we would be at the same time defining the ultimate meaning of human life.

Because of its fundamental nature, individuation eludes precise formulation, but that fact also gives us an important clue to what is involved in it. Individuation is the life-long process in a human being by which what is potential in him is brought to realization and is integrated into the wholeness of a mature life. Inherently, individuation is not a conscious process.

Studying the patterns of behavior in animal species, Jung pointed out that a psychoid proto-image, darkly unconscious and yet purposeful, guides the development of every organism. In the human species this proto-image is the Self. The Self represents the basic realities of human nature, the potentialities and the limits of human life; and since it is an image that eventually takes a psychological form, the Self is experienced as a symbol of the meaning and the goal of human existence. In a variety of archetypal forms that cover the virtually unlimited symbolism of redemption, the Self draws the person forward by relating his activities to larger contents of life beyond his immediate knowledge.

There are two aspects in the process of individuation: 1) dispositive, or the process of divesting the soul of the wrappings of a false individuation called persona, and of protecting the person against the suggestive power primordial images; 2) perfective, or the process of making as fully conscious as possible the cluster of unconscious contents and of synthetizing them with consciousness through the act of recognition.

As individuation proceeds to its goal, the person undergoes a change of personality; in Jung's term, a "rebirth" which naturally does not presuppose the alteration of the original disposition, but a transformation of general attitude. The natural transformation processes announce themselves mainly in dreams which exhibit symbols of rebirth, for it is in them that the union of conscious and unconscious is consummated: "Out of the union emerge new situations and new conscious attitudes. I have therefore called the union the 'transcendent function.' This rounding out of personality into a whole may well be the goal of any psychotherapy that claims to be more than a mere cure of symptoms (216). At this stage, the center of personality has been shifted from the ego to the self; the person has really attained the goal he was striving for, the fulfillment of his own specified nature, namely, unity and wholeness.

Jung deliberately leads his patients to individual religion as the way of salvation; that is to say, the way of individuation with the Self as the goal. The experience of finding the Self is redemption. It is connected with a subjective, redeeming feeling of great luminosity. An overriding sense of purposefulness inspires all the energies of the soul which are concentrated on the center of the personality. Jung tells us, "If one summarizes what people tell one about their experiences, it comes more or less to this; they came to themselves, they were able to reconcile themselves with themselves and they were thereby reconciled to unfavorable circumstances and events. This is practically the same thing as used to be expressed in the words: He has made his peace with God, he has sacrificed his own will by subjecting himself to the will of God" (217).

Jung tells us that all in all, it is not only more beneficial but more "correct" psychologically to explain as the "will of God" the natural forces that appear in us as instincts (218). In this way we find ourselves living in harmony with the habitus of our ancestral psychic life; that is, we function as man and woman have functioned at all times and in all places. The existence of this habitus is proof of its viability, for, if it were not viable, all those who obeyed it would long since have perished of maladaptation.

Jung maintains that modern man, as he is, separated from his divine origin and unable to balance his experiences in accordance with true values, is conscious of a deep-seated dissatisfaction and sense of frustration. This is the breeding ground for that modern complaint termed "neurosis." In essence, the neurotic person does not differ from his normal fellow. It is only that the "war with himself" is fought with greater intensity and leads to embarrassing conflicts with the outside world (219). To deal with the complexities of this situation Jung developed his method of therapy.

The doctor's task is to put the body in favorable conditions in order that the natural healing power of the organism may have its full effect. This same tendency is inherent in the psyche, too. The analyst as an ordinary person can only help his patients to remove obstacles such as deep-rooted grievances in order that the psyche may, so to speak, spontaneously regain its equilibrium. The person possesses in his psyche a very delicate instrument registering immediately whatever happens and, like a compass, it shows him when he has lost his way.

Jung states that there are in a neurosis two tendencies standing in strict opposition to one another, one of which is unconscious (220). This proposition is formulated in very general terms on purpose because he wants to stress that although the pathogenic conflict is a personal matter it is also a broadly human conflict manifesting itself in the individual, for disunity with oneself is the hall-mark of civilized man. The neurotic is only a special instance of the disunited man who ought to harmonize nature and culture with himself (221).

Neurosis is intimately bound up with the problem of our time and really represents an unsuccessful attempt on the part of the individual to solve the general problem in his own person. Neurosis is self-division. In most people the cause of the division is that the unconscious strives after its unmoral ideal which the conscious mind tries to deny.

It is under all circumstances an advantage to be in full possession of one's personality, otherwise the repressed elements will only crop up as a hindrance elsewhere, not just as some unimportant point, but at the very spot where we are most sensitive. If people can be educated to see the shadow-side of their nature clearly, it may be hoped that they will also learn to understand and love their fellow men better. A little less hypocrisy and a little more self-knowledge can only have good results in respect for our neighbor; for we are all too prone to transfer to our fellows the injustice and violence we inflict upon our own natures.

According to Jung a man is only half understood when we know how everything in him came into being. If that were all, he could just as well have been dead years ago. As a living being he is not understood, for life does not have only a yesterday, nor is it explained by reducing today to yesterday. Life has also a tomorrow, and today is understood only when we can add to our knowledge of what was yesterday the beginnings of tomorrow. This is true of all life's psychological expressions, even of pathological symptoms.

The symptoms of a neurosis are not simply the effects of long-past causes, whether infantile sexuality or the infantile urge to power. They are also attempts at a new synthesis of life, unsuccessful attempts. Yet attempts nevertheless, with a core of value and

144

meaning. They are seeds that fail to sprout owing to the inclement conditions of inner and outer nature.

The greatest and most important problems, Jung believes, are basically all insoluble; and they are so because they express the polarity immanent in every self-regulating system (222). The problems are not solved, but only transcended, a transcendence which is revealed as a raising of the level of consciousness, as a deepening of personality. "If we succeed in making the Self into a new center of gravity of the individual, then a personality arises from there that, so to speak, suffers only in the lower levels, but in the upper is peculiarly detached from every sorrowful and joyful event alike" (223). At this point, all opposites are united in the Self, which does not signify that the person is then perfect but complete, because the Self also includes evil; a completion which is not achieved without a great deal of hardship due to the tension between the ego and the Self.

In summary, opposition and duality play an important role in the Jungian development of human personality. Duality is not a luxury but a prerequisite of growth, and needs to be preserved by all means. In the last stage of the process of development, however, duality and opposition are harmonized and integrated into a higher synthesis. It is unity and wholeness, the goal of man, and this goal is intimately connected with religious content, and symbolically expressed by the archetype of the Self.

The contents of the collective unconscious appear in the beginning as autonomous complexes independent of the control of the mind and of the arbitrary power of the will. They are dangerous because, in addition to being autonomous, they are automatically projected upon external objects which absorb part of their energy. The process and techniques leading to the differentiation and assimilation of these contents by the conscious mind constitute the most important steps towards individuation. And since the archetypes of religion are the most important archetypes, religion and individuation are interwoven. Therefore the analysis of dogmas and gods is always simultaneously parallel with the steps of the process of individuation (224).

Jung's quest for mankind's common humanity, culminating in his theory of the archetype, led him inevitably into theology. It was a consistent movement, which took him from his own normative concept, the Self, to a consideration of Christology, the normative concept of Christian theology. Jung held that Christ represents a concrete embodiment of the God-man relation inherent in the nature of all men.

For Jung, the life of Jesus Christ can be understood as the personal and historical realization of the God-man archetype. Jesus Christ lived a concrete and unique life which had, at the same time, an archetypal character. Ultimately, every human life is archetypal in

146

its collective bases. Hence the clue to understanding Jung's thought is found in a bipolar movement, from microcosm to macrocosm, from the "other" prior to the self to the "other" common with the self, from potential to actual.

In Jesus Christ, we find that the archetype as potential becomes actual in his life. The archetype as indefinite and illimitable became definite and concretely embodied in him. The archetype as universal became unique. As eternal, as the sense of an ever-present reality, it became unitemporal. The archetype as collective became individuated. We can speak of the self-transcending side of the archetype in Jesus Christ as the "Son of God." We can speak of the personal aspects of his selfhood as the "Son of Man."

Jung denies categorically that Christ has any objective reality as a divine person. What is divine in the mystery of Christ is what is universally human. Every God is impersonal and universally valid. It is a "spirit," as is shown quite clearly by the original Christian tradition. The "divine" simply covers whatever is not individual. It represents whatever is valid universally, which is the same thing as saying, universally human. God is everything in man that transcends the ego. As Jung sees only this kind of immanence, the divine can only be a universal or "collective" psychic reality.

Jung tells us that there can be no doubt that the original Christian conception of the imago Dei embodied in Christ meant an all-embracing totality that even includes the animal side of man.

Nevertheless the Christ-symbol lacks wholeness in the modern psychological sense, since it does not include the dark side of things but specifically excludes it in the form of a Luciferien opponent (225). Although the exclusion of the power of evil was something the Christian consciousness was well aware of, all it lost in effect was an insubstantial shadow for, through the doctrine of the privatio boni first propounded by Origen, evil was characterized as a mere diminution of good and thus deprived of substance. According to the teachings of the Church, evil is simply "the accidental lack of perfection." This assumption resulted in the proposition "All good from God, all evil from man."

Although the attributes of Christ undoubtedly mark him out as an embodiment of the Self, looked at from the psychological angle he corresponds to only one-half of the archetype. The other half appears in the anti-Christ. The latter is just as much a manifestation of the Self, except that he consists of its dark aspect (226). Both are Christian symbols, and they have the same meaning as the image of the Savior crucified between two thieves. This great symbol tells us that the progressive development of consciousness leads to an ever more menacing awareness of the conflict and involves nothing less than a crucifixion of the ego, its agonizing suspension between irreconcilable opposites.

Jung maintains that in unconscious humanity there is a latent seed that corresponds to the prototype Jesus. Just as the man Jesus became conscious only through the light that emanated from the higher Christ and separated the natures in him, so the seed in unconscious humanity is awakened by the light emanating from Jesus, and is thereby impelled to a similar discrimination of opposites. This view is entirely in accord with the psychological fact that the archetypal image of the Self has been shown to occur in dreams even when no such conceptions exist in the conscious mind of the dreamer.

If one inclines to regard the archetype of the Self as the real agent and hence take Christ as a symbol of the Self, one must bear in mind that there is a considerable difference between perfection and completeness (227). The Christ-image is as good as perfect while the archetype denotes completeness but is far from being perfect. It is a paradox, a statement about something indescribable and transcendental. Accordingly the realization of the Self, which would logically follow from a recognition of its supremacy, leads to a fundamental conflict, to a real suspension between opposites, and to an approximate state of wholeness that lacks perfection.

Jung suggests that the striving after a sense of perfection is not only legitimate but is inborn in man as a peculiarity which provides civilization with one of its strongest roots (228). This striving is so powerful, even, that it can turn into a passion that draws everything into its service. Natural as it is to seek perfection in one way or another, the archetype fulfills itself in completeness. Where the archetype predominates, completeness is forced upon as against all our conscious strivings, in accordance with the archaic nature of the archetype. The individual may strive after perfection but must suffer from the opposite of his intentions for the sake of his completeness.

Christ is the still living myth of our culture. He is our culture hero who, regardless of his historical existence, embodies the myth of the divine primordial man, the mystic Adam. Christ exemplifies the archetype of the Self. He represents a totality of a divine or heavenly kind, a glorified man, a son of God unspotted by sin. As the second Adam he corresponds to the first Adam before the Fall, when the latter was still a pure image of God, of which Tertullian says, "And this therefore is to be considered as the image of God in man, that the human spirit has the same motions and senses as God has, though not in the same way as God has them" (229).

Christ symbolizes the libido, which engenders life beyond death. Because he concretizes psychic energy in a particularly striking way, Christian believers look to him as a personal example that they themselves can follow. Without realizing it, they recognize him as the ideal projection of the psychic energy that is at work in the depths of their own being. They submit to him as a person, believing him to be an objective reality, because he is in fact simply the most precious part of themselves.

B. The Catholic Response

Judging from magisterial documents, we may conclude that systematics is deemed infinitely more significant for the Catholic than is the development of the behavioral component of religious life. Because moral theology has the kind of history that I earlier alluded to, we find scattered in Catholic writings a moral paradigm that is not nearly as well molded as are the elements of belief. There is diversity, fragmentation, and even silence in dealing with questions of Christian behavior. We must keep this situation in mind as we examine the Catholic counterpart to Jung's view of human structure and behavior.

In attempting to present the Catholic position, we shall rely on the teaching of St. Thomas. Bear in mind that we are keeping to the 'natural' parameters that restricts this entire study. Our whole analysis of human experience bears witness that there is in the human person an absolute exigence for progress which demands of him, since it is not possible for him to perfect himself by his own powers, that he open his mind to the mystery of this transcendence on which he and the world depend. There is in man the aspiration to be like God, and this aspiration is what Christian metaphysics and theology have keenly analyzed for a long time (230).

For Thomas, all creation is lifted up by an immense urge which, from its very depths, impels it toward God. It is shot through and through by a dynamism of structure, by a love of nature which

151

relates it to its source. Man does not escape this vast aspiration which elevates creation toward God. He discovers in his deepest consciousness his existential relation to Him who has given him being, and who from the interior recalls to him this upsurge of nature so utterly irrepressible, of which he is not the master, and which is at the very source of his being, and by that very fact, of his mind.

According to Thomas, man's intelligence is open to all being, it has an unlimited capacity, and God alone can fill this desire of all being. This will, that is, the dynamism of an intelligent being, is also open to the unlimited horizon of the good. Made for universal good, nothing consequently can wholly satisfy it but God, the universal Good.

From the fact of this opening to the mystery of all being, there is in the heart of the person an aspiration for a perfection of self which is of the spiritual order, of a dimension even divine. It is clear that one has not said everything of the human being when, with Aristotle, he has defined him as a rational animal. His specific dimension thus set forth does not exhaust his grandeur.

This astonishing dimension of the person is what St. Thomas calls the natural desire of seeing God. It is in it that the great mystery of the person consists, a mystery which we have never fully explained, before which we can assert a priori that all our efforts will fail, for it is the mystery of person as spirit, of his soul considered not so much as form of the body, but as spirit.

This natural desire of seeing God is a desire of the will to seek the good proper to the intellect. To possess God by intelligence is for the person the object of love, and since the object of this love is not present in this life, love tends toward it and desires it. It is a natural desire because it flows from the intellectual nature as such, commanded by a natural knowledge. Knowing God by reason, we aspire to know Him in His essence, in Himself.

Jung's conception of the person also has a certain grandeur and depth. It can help an anxious, even a deeply disturbed individual to recover some degree of peace and inner harmony, to accept himself and others --- a discreet readiness to accept himself and others. This lies half-way between man's primitive needs and the highest demands of the human spirit, and it can give back courage to those defeated by the tension of their life or who are depressed and uneasy, constricted by a narrow code of conduct or the artificial "persona" they have created.

It releases tension and may well be an effective treatment for anxiety. But it does not touch the Christian idea of holiness. It may serve as a stepping stone toward a higher, more balanced self-mastery, toward a more personal pledging of the reconquered "Self." From the Christian perspective, such therapy will always be inadequate without involving love, which hardly appears at all in the Jungian system. For communion with the universe and with others, of which Jung speaks, is made through the medium of symbols rather than by an act of charity and self-giving.

Holiness, for the Catholic, consists in union with God. It implies two things: being cleansed of anything that can sully, and adhering staunchly to God through love. Sanctity has unlimited degrees, for everyone is capable of yet greater holiness. Holiness is usually considered as being common (ordinary) or heroic. It is only in speaking of heroic holiness that we can relate to Jung's suggestion of Christian perfection (231). The ordinary Catholic is called to ordinary holiness, not perfection.

Jung's psychology sees its significance in restoring the connection in the total psychic structure between the unconscious and consciousness, in healing the soul, making it whole. This is a problem which in periods of collective culture devolved on the redemptive religions, but which today seeks its solution in individualism. The individual must face his own religious problem; that is, the problem of giving birth to the expression of his own supremely personal nature in the unifying symbol of the Self. Our soul is strong enough to create new religious forms and symbols, which do justice to the variety and character of the individual. From this point of view our age is only at the beginning of a new spiritual culture.

Jung tells us that we have to rely on the curative powers inherent in the patient's own nature, regardless of whether the ideas that emerge agree with any known creed or philosophy. "My empirical material seems to include a bit of everything --- it is an assortment of primitive, Western and Oriental ideas (232). There is scarcely any myth whose echoes are not heard, not any heresy that has not contributed an occasional oddity. The deeper, collective layers of the human psyche must surely be of a like nature" (233).

Any Catholic has to be surprised by the selection of religious personalities that Jung calls upon to demonstrate his positions. For instance, Jung, in harmony with his dualistic premises, contrasts Tertullian and Origen and suggests that they are the pair who 1) established the overbearing rationalism of Catholicism (Origen) and 2) elevated the emotional or feeling component in religious behavior (Tertullian). But Jung fails to mention that the Catholic documents show ample repudiation of certain views of Origen.

Origenistic views are condemned by St. Anastasius I (398-401), by Pope Vigilius in 537, by the Second Council of Constantinople in 553, and by the Lateran Council of 649 (234). While we do not feel that these condemnations allow us to ignore the significance of Origen in the development of Christian theology, it is misleading to suggest that there is no problem in wholeheartedly accepting his views.

Jung has great admiration for Tertullian's "I believe because it is absurd." He says of Tertullian that, thanks to the acuteness of his mind, he saw through the poverty of philosophical and gnostic knowledge, and contemptuously rejected it. He invoked against it the testimony of his own inner world, his own inner realities, which were one with his faith. In shaping and developing these realities he became the creator of those abstract conceptions which, according to Jung, still underlie the Catholic system of today (235). The irrational inner reality had for him an essentially dynamic nature; it was his principle, his foundation in fact of the world and of all collectively valid and rational science and philosophy.

Jung depicts Origen as the absolute opposite of Tertullian. He was a great scholar who did not cut himself off from the influence of gnosticism. It is, Jung says, entirely characteristic that Tertullian should perform the sacrificium intellectus, whereas Origen was led to the sacrificium phalli, because the Christian process demands a complete abolition of the sensual tie to the object; in other words, it demands the sacrifice of the hitherto most valued function, the dearest possession, the strongest instinct. Considered biologically, the sacrifice serves the interests of domestication, but psychologically it opens a door for new possibilities of spiritual development through the dissolution of old ties.

The same comment made about Origen applies to Meister Eckhart. Jung does not avert to the fact that Eckhart must be read with certain care since a number of his positions were examined and condemned in the document "In agro dominico," March 27, 1329. Some of the articles were deemed heretical while others were thought to be "evil-sounding, rash and suspected of heresy" (236).

It is specifically the Christian mystical tradition, represented most characteristically by Meister Eckhart, that Jung holds up as normative for the Christian experience, but to do so is incorrect and inadequate to the rich diversity of experiences possible within the Christian faith tradition.

In agreement with Eckhart, the goal of Jung's redemptive therapy is God. But this God is in the soul and to confirm his view Jung quotes from Meister Eckhart: "God must forever be born in the soul" (237). God, in Jung's view, arises in man through individuation. "We must direct our patients to the place where the One, the All-Uniting arises in them." All the forces of the soul are concentrated in the Self, the soul is made "whole" --- that is redemption according to Jung's theory of the soul. "The journey through the spiritual history of mankind has the purpose of restoring man as a whole by rousing the memories of the blood" (238).

Jung believes that the Trinity, as expressed by the Christian faith in the form of Father, Son and Holy Spirit, is best regarded as a projection three states through which every person passes. The person of the Father is an expression of the original state of non-differentiation. At this first stage, non-differentiated being is identified absolutely with the family or group. The child, or the primitive, thinks, lives, feels, judges, through and in the family or group, and is quite unable to take up any objective attitude toward it.

According to Analytical knowledge the following development takes place in the life of the individual. At first the child is united to his parents by the projection of the archetypes on to them. Gradually there develops a personal relationship. Father and Mother become Priest and Mother Church, to which is added the spiritual aspect of the Mother as the Virgin.

Thus in relation to religion, in relation to the Church, and in relation to God, the ordinary man or woman is kept firmly in the state of a child. This state is of the greatest value for two reasons; 1) because the state of being a "child" is the necessary prerequisite for entry into the Kingdom of Heaven and, 2) because those who are living in the world need to have the archetypal form of the unconscious held or contained somewhere. Within the Church they are held through regular services and rituals prescribed by her. Thus, though the main activity of the ordinary man is in the world, he never loses touch with the archetypal images, projected into the rituals at the center of which is the Mass. The Church, therefore, stands between the ego and divine mysteries in the same relation as the soul stands between the ego and the mystical communion with God.

Before long, however, it discovers that it possess an independent personal existence and inevitably tries to emancipate itself. It turns its back on its mother's love, throws off its father's authority, and hurls itself into a battle for its own personality in the external world. It thus enters upon the second stage --- represented, according to Jung, by the Son --- and tries to free itself from its mother and father and the rest of the family. This kind of affirmation through opposition is necessary for anyone who is determined to discover his own personality and if the process is hindered, either by dominating parents or through failure on the part of the adolescent himself, his world will harden at the infantile stage and be dominated by the figure of his father. This second period is therefore usually characterized by an exclusive tendency towards liberation and self-affirmation.

This exclusive line of development needs to be transcended in its turn, and in the third stage the grown man should unite the two preceding stages by realizing that his independence is no more absolute than the other values in his life and has no meaning unless he is prepared to submit freely to a reality that transcends him. He thus returns to the totality he had left behind him, not through any childish abdication of responsibility but as a result of an adult submission. As the first stage is dominated by the Father and the second by the Son so the third, which unites the first two is dominated by the Spirit, the link between Father and Son.

According to Jung, then, the archetype that lies behind the Trinity is in fact the psychic reality of the three stages that man goes through on the way to full development. Seen from this angle the Trinity is the transposition of a subjective reality to a "metaphysical" plane --- a plane "situated outside the subject." From his observations Jung concluded that ternary symbols generally only express a state of partial perfection. He found this surprising, and the question it led him to ask was whether Western man had omitted some essential element from his representation of God. The answer he finally gave to this question was yes.

In point of fact Jung had been strongly impressed by the part played in the process of individuation by evil, and he was astonished to find no trace of evil in the representation of God, who was always conceived of as the Supreme Good. He decided that this suppression must be the result of a generalized repression.

In Jung's view the emphasis on the sovereign goodness of God, whose Fatherhood was revealed by the Son, inevitably led Christian theology to remove the power of the Prince of Darkness out of range of God's immediate control. Christian thinkers contented themselves with stating that at the end of time the divine omnipotence would manifest itself in a resounding victory that would show Lucifer and his crew the futility of their endeavors.

Jung is afraid that by thus dissociating good and evil they created an irresolvable dualism, all the more dangerous from the fact that it remained unconscious. He says that this divorce between good and evil on the objective plan of divinity is symptomatic of a psychic dissociation within man himself, who is no longer prepared to recognize the lower part of his being as part of himself.

The Trinitarian argument of Jung points to a weak spot in his thinking on the correlation of Catholic systematics and its psychological counterpart. What he postulates in fact as the basis for his whole line of reasoning is that God is to be identified with the ideal image that man should, and does, form of himself and then projects into the supra-human or metaphysical order. This takes Jung a thousand miles from the actual dogmas themselves (239). For, among others, the Trinitarian dogma never mentions man's idea of God; it is entirely concerned with God's being, as a thing revealed. Nothing drawn from any idea of God can help to thrown any light on God's being.

It is obvious that the problem lies in Jung's failure to make a distinction between what is natural and what is supernatural. Every component of Catholicism is a natural one insofar as Jung is concerned. Catholicism, on the other hand, distinguishes between what is natural and what is supernatural. For the Catholic, the Church and the Trinity are revealed, are supernatural; for Jung they are simply psychological components of the human person and he analyses them as such. To argue the point against Jung is counter-productive because by his method of psychological reductionism the Church's arguments are themselves further proof of the point he wishes to make.

Theologians, even those sympathetic toward Jung's work, are inevitably critical of his tendency to assimilate religious practice to psychotherapy. The priest's role, they insist, is entirely different from the therapist's. Whereas to Jung a great healing factor in psychotherapy is the doctor's personality, the Christian director does not offer himself as a support but points instead to Christ or God. And whereas the analyst is concerned with bringing to consciousness unconscious tendencies, for which the patient cannot be held responsible, the priest in the sacrament of confession (penance or reconciliation) mediates God's forgiveness of intentional conscious acts, of which the sinner has repented.

In the early days Jung expostulated against the identification of psychological analysis and confession. But as he gradually discovered that the various religions provide mankind with "the great psychotherapeutic systems of the past" he grew more and more interested in confession. Soon he was having no hesitation in saying that psycho-analysis was a logical development of confession and that his method, like Freud's, was based on the practice of confession. In The Practice of Psychotherapy Jung tells us that "the first beginnings of all analytical treatment of the soul are to be found in its prototype, the confessional (240). Since, however, the two have no direct causal connection, but rather grow from a common irrational psychic root, it is difficult for an outsider to see at once the relation between the groundwork of psychoanalysis and the religious institution of the confession."

But confession and analysis are at opposite poles. Confession means forgiveness of intentional conscious acts that have been repented of. Analysis brings into consciousness unconscious tendencies for which the person concerned cannot be held responsible. If we ignore these radical differences and try to reconcile confession and analysis simply because they have the structural element of acknowledgment in common, we stray beyond the field of phenomenology, for phenomenology is based on the comparison of structures that are identical in meaning, and the meaning of the acknowledgment made in confession is not at all the same thing as the meaning of that which is made in psychotherapy.

One of the greatest differences between Jung and the Christian tradition is, clearly, that Jung is operating without the transcendental element. As David Cox points out, Christian faith is "faith in a guide, who will lead one to the goal of life, whereas the faith for which Jung asks is faith that one will come to the goal without a guide, or that there is a guide although one is not aware of being guided, and there is very little likeness between the two" (241).

For the most part Jung deprecates the transcendental element in Christianity on two rather different grounds; its childishness and its remoteness. Under the first heading he writes that unlike the man of the East, who knows that redemption depends on the "words" a person devotes to himself, we in the West are still so uneducated that we need laws from without and a taskmaster of Father above (242); and under the second, that if a god is accepted who is absolute and beyond all human experience "He leaves me cold" (243).

Michael Fordham claims that it is Jung's achievement that he succeeded in bringing Eastern mysticism and Western science closer together; he finds that if science is used to study the psyche, we arrive at the position of conflict between the opposites comprising spirit and instinct. If we are able to balance these and maintain an equilibrium, a synthesis gradually occurs. It is the synthetic process which is the same in the East as in the West.

Jung did an exhaustive study of Eastern religious symbolism and there are those who claim that his writings indicate that he subjected those religions to the same analysis and to the same criticism as their Western counterparts. Whether Jung's views of the Eastern religions vis-a-vis Western religions are correct is open to question.

For instance, Jung states that unfortunately our Western mind has never yet devised a concept, nor even a name, for the union of opposites through the middle path, that most fundamental item of inward experience, which could respectably be set against the Chinese concept of Tao. "It is at once the most individual fact and the most universal, the most legitimate fulfillment of the meaning of the individual's life" (244). Though it may not be expressed in the same way, it seems that Jung overlooks the concept of the golden mean. That concept certainly steers us to a middle path and its origins can be traced back to the Greek foundations of our civilization.

Mircea Eliade has prefaced one of his more recent books by recalling Whitehead's familiar remark that the history of Western philosophy is nothing more than a series of footnotes to Plato, but adding that the wisdom of such "splendid isolation" has become increasingly questionable in modern epoch (245). Eliade's concern is, of course, with the bearing of primitive and Eastern religions upon the religions and intellectual formations of the West, but it is important to note that he has again and again counted the discoveries of depth psychology as one of several extremely important "outsiders" that have invaded the once closed field of the Western consciousness.

Jung's criticism of "the great philosophical systems of the East" applies to "all the dogmatic religions of the West." Jung strips both of their metaphysical wrappings in order to make them objects of psychology. "In this way I can at least get something comprehensible out of them and can avail myself of it. Moreover I learn psychological conditions and processes which before were veiled in symbols and out of reach of my understanding. My admiration for the great Eastern philosophers is as great as my attitude towards them is irreverent. I suspect them of being symbolic psychologists to whom no greater wrong could be done than to take them literally" (246).

Finally, for Jung, images dwell somehow, hidden from ordinary consciousness, in every man's mind; they are archetypes not of reality but of mental operations. It did not occur to him that in fact one can, and probably with better reason, explain the recurrence of symbols as the result of objective rather than subjective factors. It is conceivable that certain common data of experience and certain forms and shapes that come readily to mind are, by their own nature, symbols; they reveal a "world of meaning." In other words, symbols are not so much created as discovered. Both natural phenomena and artifacts may prove to be symbolic in themselves. One of the commonest symbols is the wheel, and another is the door. Both are artifacts and were certainly not invented as symbols.

166

The Conclusion

Several years before his death, with a realization that comes only to those who know they may be uttering final life-reflections, Jung stated that " My *raison d'etre* consists in coming to terms with that indefinable Being we call 'God'" (247). This synoptic analysis has taken several of Jung's major themes dealing with his coming to terms with 'God' and has contrasted them with corresponding formulations articulated by the Catholic magisterium or theological positions flowing from them.

Several conclusions have emerged. The primary one concern Jung's close affinity with the premises of modernism. It would be shallow to simply blanket Jung with that charge, but from a magisterial perspective, Jung has made the thinking of modernism part of his own.

Second, Jung allows for a model of the human person that assumes, in concert with much of modern psychology, that decisions are made on the basis of the dynamic interplay of the conscious and the unconscious, the rational and the irrational. The magisterium, in accordance with the Greek model, favors the rational mode of decision making with almost exclusive emphasis on the conscious.

Third, Jung reduces all of what we can know about reality to the natural plane. Though Catholicism is complimented by Jung's compatibility with natural theology, it disagrees with his reduction of certain supernatural beliefs to natural phenomena.

Fourth, though the magisterium would afford Jung a standing ovation for his near preoccupation with religious matters, a scrutiny of his works by Catholic authors lead to a uniform conclusion: Jung uses theological vocabulary to discard or emend the ideas held by theology itself. From the magisterium's point of view, one could always begin a religious journey with Jung, but one could just as assuredly never expect to travel with him to the journey's conclusion.

In one of his writings, Jung states, "Not only do I leave the door open for the Christian message, but I consider it of central importance for Western man. It needs, however, to be seen in a new light, in accordance with the changes wrought by the contemporary spirit. Otherwise it stands apart from the times, and has no effect on man's wholeness" (248). The concluding pages of this paper review the highlights of Jung's spirit, the magisterium's reactions to those highlights, and a final word indicates how Jung may be helpful to Catholic thinking, no matter what problems he presents.

It has been suggested throughout this study that the magisterium of the Catholic Church would find a 'psychological modernism' as the basis for Jung's presuppositions. Jung shows a pronounced relationship to the modernist heresy, a heresy which arose in the very bosom of the Church at the beginning of this century under the influence of modern philosophy and criticism, with the pretense of elevating and saving the Christian religion and the Catholic Church by means of a radical renovation.

The magisterial Church views modernism as a hybrid amalgamation of principles that coincidentally form the backbone of Jung's paradigm. The components include: 1) Kantian agnosticism, which combines subjectivism, phenomenalism, and relativism, depreciating rational knowledge; 2) immanentism, according to which human consciousness bears in itself, virtually, every truth, even divine, which is developed under the stimulus of the religious sense; and 3) radical evolutionism, according to which true reality is not being, but becoming, both within and outside man.

The consequences of this heresy, insofar as they affect a religious perspective are: 1) the impossibility of demonstrating the existence of a personal God, distinct from the world or the human psyche, and 2) religion and revelation as natural products of our consciousness, dogma being its provisional expression, subject to continual evolution.

Jung concurs in the rejection of the genuine possibility of an intellectual statement of the reality to which dogma refers, a statement which would belong to the constitution of religious experience itself. For Modernism, the conceptual intellectual proposition which constitutes dogma is not merely "inadequate" to the reality signified, nor is it an "analogical" statement which originates and directs man into mystery utterly beyond his scope. Dogma is seen as secondary and derivative as compared with religious experience. Viewed positively, dogma, according to Modernism, is a derivative expression of religious experience, unavoidably necessary for the religious community, but always subject to revision or even to change into its contrary, and religious experience itself if given an immanentist interpretation.

A second major concern is the understanding of natural theology as perceived by Jung and by Catholicism. For Jung, every religious component is a development from its natural manifestation in the psyche. Ultimately every religious idea can be reduced to psychological phenomena. For the Catholic, as for every Christian, there are certain revelations from God that constitute a transcendental dimension of religion which cannot be found in a natural theology. These opposing views account for the discrepancy between Jung and Catholicism.

Catholicism sees the Trinity as a revelation of a supernatural character, on a level beyond the reach of the person's highest natural powers. The Trinity, for Jung, is an unfolding of natural archetypal powers and lies within the potential unconsciousness of every person caught up in the individuation process. We see the audacious creativity of Jung in his analysis that a full understanding of the psychic phenomena would lead to a quaternity rather than a trinity.

In natural theology we see the immediate affinity that attracted Jung to Catholicism, though we can see as well that Jung's discounting of the supernatural causes a serious rift in the psychological analysis of religion. There is a more readily available channel of communication between Jung and Catholicism because of the natural theology component, a component which suggests that psychology as well as theology knows that the person is made in the image of God.

The subject matter of Jung's science is the psyche and its goal the Self. In terms traditional since Augustine, there is no more acceptable model for the divinity than the Self; no more perspicuous image of the transcendent Creator than the creature who is creative in his own right. Furthermore, Jung respects the negative properties of theology, since the Self remains transcendent to the science. For him the Self is its goal rather than its subject.

Transcendence means the concrete resolution of social, economic, and political problems as well as spiritual and psychic wholeness. Transcendence becomes, in fact, a general category, utilized by many diverse disciplines to mean essentially the same thing, that is, the total fulfillment of human life.

The theologian, then, when he speaks of transcendence in this-worldly manner, shares the same moral objectives as the humanistic and social sciences. He is not describing a world foreign to the ordinary experiences of the common man, a world "up there" inhabited by divine and supernatural beings. He is pointing to a fundamental human drive, that urge within the person for the enhancement and completion of human personality, the amelioration of those tensions and differences within his world that inhibit the perfect fulfillment of the human condition (249).

Of course, one cannot claim that theology has a more valid concept of transcendence than the other disciplines, because the claim of theology must be empirically verified; one can say it is evident that theology is not an irrelevant and antihumanistic discipline. Rather it appears that theology has entered the intellectual arena once again with great vitality and forcefulness, and it does so claiming to be an accurate interpreter of the human condition. But even more so, theology asserts that it can provide an adequate resolution to the human dilemma, the inherent desire of the person for wholeness and perfection.

We have already indicated that Jung introduces a note of confusion into Catholic morality when he chooses to contrast its 'perfection' with his wholeness. Sanctification, not perfection, is the Catholic goal of human life. Perfection is always a relative concept since it is admitted by nearly every theological school of Catholic morality to be an unattainable goal. The idea of spiritual growth having a terminal point in this life may be suggested by certain Eastern schools of spirituality, but it is not a component of Catholicism.

Perhaps the idea of "mastering" a spiritual objective accounts for Jung's ambivalence toward the significance of the Church and community or fellowship. Jung favors ideals of self-development, including "widened or deepened consciousness," saying that exclusive reliance on the principle of love is apt to bring about "a collective culture in which the individual threatens to be swallowed up, and individual values are depreciated on principle." Though Jung's therapeutic technique is enhanced in Catholic eyes by its following the Christian pattern of life, death and resurrection, it must be similarly noticed that his lack of emphasis on loving relationships assumes disturbing importance.

Jung is the spokesman of the attitude that has been prevalent during the last half century. Slowly but surely he has rediscovered the religious and the sacred and got rid of an overweening rationalism. On the other hand, religious feeling, with all its irrationality, has fascinated him to such an extent that he has banished all the intellectual elements from it. There are no rational statements about God, no products of directed thinking with which it can be compared. Thus, the very possibility that religion could develop into an adult, rational, voluntary relationship --- such as Jung may hope from his patient's imago having been analyzed --- is a priori excluded.

According to Jung, primitive man impresses us so strongly with his subjectivity that we should really have guessed long ago that myths refer to something psychic. His knowledge of nature is essentially the language and outer dress of an unconscious psychic process (250). But the very fact that this process is unconscious gives us the reason why the person has thought of everything except the psyche in his attempts to explain myths. He simply didn't know that the psyche contains all the images that have ever given rise to myths, and that our unconscious is an acting and suffering subject with an inner drama which the primitive person rediscovers, by means of analogy, in the processes of nature both great and small.

It is understandable why psychology appeared so late and is thus a very young science. For it demands a certain degree of consciousness to recognize the reality of the soul and the images that flow from it. We live in and through the soul and are so wrapped up in it that we do not notice it at all. It is, in the Kantian sense, a phenomenon. To recognize the difference between the thing-in-itself and the thing-as-it-appears requires a degree of psychic consciousness and differentiation which mankind only reaches quite late and which is by no means given to all even today.

For Jung, that people should succumb to these eternal images is entirely normal, in fact it is what these images are for. They are meant to attract, to convince, to fascinate, and to overpower. They are created out of the primal stuff of revelation and reflect the ever-unique experience of divinity. That is why they always give the person a premonition of the divine while at the same time safeguarding him from immediate experience of it. Thanks to the labors of the human spirit over the centuries, these images have become embedded in a comprehensive system of thought that ascribes an order to the world, and are at the same time represented by a mighty, far-spread, and venerable institution called the Church.

According to Jung, dogma takes the place of the collective unconscious by formulating its contents on a grand scale (251). The Catholic way of life is completely unaware of psychological problems in this sense (252). Almost the entire life of the collective unconscious has been channeled into the dogmatic archetypal ideas and flows along like a well-controlled stream in the symbolism of creed and ritual. It manifests itself in the inwardness of the Catholic psyche.

The collective unconscious, as we understand it today, was never a matter of "psychology," for before the Christian Church existed there were the antique mysteries, and these reach back into the grey mists of neolithic history. Mankind has never lacked powerful images to lend magical aid against all the uncanny things that live in the depths of the psyche. Always the figures of the unconscious were expressed in protecting and healing images and in this way were expelled from the psyche into cosmic space.

Mankind came to assume that "without" and "objective" were one and the same thing, as were "subjective" and "within." Jung believed that they were by no means synonymous and that there was something as objective within the human being as great as the objective without, and that people were subject to two great objective worlds, the physical world without and a world within, invisible except to the sensibilities of the imagination. Jung felt that meaning could be restored to religion only by enabling it to become the living experience for all people that it had been to him since childhood. At the same time it was only be re-dedication of science to the service also of meaning that religion could receive an essential empiricism and the two join in an overall purpose wherein they should never have been allowed to divide against each other.

Archetypal images are so packed with meaning in themselves that people never think of asking what they really do mean. As Jung sees it, that the gods die from time to time is due to our sudden discovery that they do not mean anything, that they are made by human hands, useless idols of wood and stone (253). In reality, however, he has merely discovered that up till then he has never thought about his images at all. And when he starts thinking about them, he does so with the help of what he calls "reason" --- which in point of fact is nothing more, for Jung, than the sum-total of all his prejudices and myopic views.

From one point of view it could almost be said that in the case of those moderns who proclaim that they are nonreligious, religion is "eclipsed" in the darkness of their unconscious --- which means, too, that in such people the possibility of reintegrating a religious vision of life lies at a great depth. Or, from the Christian point of view, it could also be said that non-religion is equivalent to a new "fall" of the person --- in other words, that non-religious men and women have lost the capacity to live religion consciously, and hence to understand and assume it; but that, in their deepest being, they still retain a memory of it, as, after the first "fall," their ancestors, the primordial man, retained intelligence enough to enable him to rediscover the traces of God that are visible in the world. After the first "fall" the religious sense descended to the level of the "divided consciousness;" now, after the second, it has fallen even further, into the depths of the unconscious; it has been "forgotten" (254).

Jung rejects many contemporary psychological statements disparaging the concept of the soul. Modern psychology has the greatest difficulty in vindicating the human soul's right to existence, and in making it credible that the soul is a mode of being with properties that can be investigated, and therefore a suitable object for scientific study; that it is not something attached to an outside, but has an autonomous inside, too, and a life of its own; that it is not just an ego-consciousness, but an existent which in all essentials can only be inferred indirectly. To people who think otherwise, the myths and dogma of the Church are bound to appear as a collection of absurd and impossible statements.

For Jung, modern rationalism is a process of sham enlightenment and even prides itself morally on its iconoclastic tendencies (255). Most people are satisfied with the not very intelligent view that the whole purpose of dogma is to state a flat impossibility. That it could be the symbolic expression of a definite idea with a definite content is something that occurs to hardly anybody. For how can one possibly know what that idea really is! And what "I" do not know simply does not exist. The conclusion: there is no non-conscious psyche.

According to Jung, we are so used to the idea that psychic events are willful and arbitrary products, or even the inventions of a human creator, that we can hardly rid ourselves of the prejudiced view that the psyche and its contents are nothing but our own arbitrary invention or the more or less illusory product of supposition and judgment. The fact is that certain ideas exist almost everywhere and at all times and can even spontaneously create themselves quite independently of migration and tradition. They are not made by the individual, they just happen to him --- they even force themselves on his consciousness. This is not Platonic philosophy but empirical psychology.

Our modern attitude looks back arrogantly upon the mists of superstition and of medieval or primitive credulity, entirely forgetting that we carry the whole living past in the storeys of the skyscraper of rational consciousness. Without the lower storeys our mind is suspended in midair. No wonder it gets nervous. The true history of the mind is not preserved in learned volumes but in the living psychic organism of every individual (256).

Dogma expresses the psyche more completely than a scientific theory, for the latter gives expression to and formulates the conscious mind alone. Furthermore, a theory can do nothing except formulate a living thing in abstract terms. Dogma, on the contrary, aptly expresses the living process of the unconscious in the form of the drama of repentance, sacrifice and redemption.

To gain an understanding of religious matters, probably all that is left us today is the psychological approach. That is why Jung takes these thought-forms that have become historically fixed, tries to

179

melt them down and pours them into molds of immediate experience. It is certainly a difficult undertaking to discover connecting links between dogma and immediate experience of psychological archetypes, but a study of the natural symbols of the unconscious gives us the necessary raw material.

Although dogma, like mythology in general, expresses the quintessence of inner experience and thus formulates the operative principles of the objective psyche, i.e., the collective unconscious, it does so by making use of a language and outlook that have become alien to our present way of thinking. The word "dogma" has even acquired a somewhat unpleasant sound and frequently serves merely to emphasize the rigidity of a prejudice. For most people living in the West, it has lost its meaning as a symbol for a virtually unknowable and yet "actual" --- i.e., operative --- fact.

Jung maintains that even in theological circles any real discussion of dogma has as good as ceased until the recent papal declaration (257), a sign that the symbol has begun to fade, if it is not already withered. This is a dangerous development for our psychic health, as we know of no other symbol that better expresses the world of the unconscious. More and more people then begin looking round for exotic ideas in the hope of finding a substitute, for example in India.

It may seem strange that a physician and psychologist should be so insistent about dogma. But Jung emphasizes it, and for the same reasons that once moved the alchemist to attach special important to his "theoria." His doctrine is at the heart of the symbolism of unconscious processes, just as the dogmas are a condensation or distillation of "sacred history," of the myths of the divine being and his deeds. If we wish to understand what alchemical doctrine means, we must go back to the historical as well as the individual phenomenology of the symbols, and if we wish to gain a closer understanding of dogma, we must perforce consider first the myths of the near and middle East that underlie Christianity, and then the whole of mythology as the expression of a universal disposition in the person.

For Jung the bridge from dogma to the inner experience of the individual has broken down. Instead, dogma is "believed;" it is hypostatized, as some Protestants hypostatize the Bible, illegitimately making it the supreme authority, regardless of its contradictions and controversial interpretations. Dogma no longer formulates anything, no longer expresses anything; it has become a tenet to be accepted in and for itself, with no basis in any experience that would demonstrate its truth.

Indeed, faith has itself become that experience. The faith of a man like Paul, who had never seen our Lord in the flesh, could still appeal to the overwhelming apparition on the road to Damascus and to the revelation of the gospel in a kind of ecstasy. Similarly, the faith of the men and women of antiquity and of the medieval Christian never ran counter to the consensus omnium but was on the contrary supported by it. All this has completely changed in the last three hundred years.

Jung's interest in the old alchemists' symbolism is fundamentally psychological and the same must be said of his interest in symbolism. All the references to alchemy in his studies of the Trinity, the Mass, Christ, etc., show this beyond all doubt. It is dangerous to speak of Jung as having a genuine interest in religion for its own sake. It is safer to say that he values religion because it provides an unfailing source of symbols.

Dogma, Jung says, expresses an irrational whole by means of imagery and reflects the spontaneous and autonomous activity of the objective psyche, the unconscious. Dogmas are valuable insofar as they are rooted in religious experience. Experience, and not faith, is their starting point. This experience is at least in part irrational, and if dogmas become too external and void of experience, then they are completely obsolete, no more than relics of the past.

Myths and dogmas are not only expressions of the contents of the unconscious, but of what, perhaps, is more important; its motions and life. "Myths and dogmas are self-portraits of the movement of the libido. Thus the sun, the snake, the fire, the horse are its symbols" (258). For instance, the course of the sun in myth is an expression of the movement of the libido; the sun's nocturnal journey across the heavens means progression of the libido. Therefore, on the Christian level dogmas are symbolic expressions of the life of the unconscious of the Christian person.

For instance, the mystery of the Eucharist, Jung says, transforms the soul of the empirical man into his totality, symbolically expressed by Christ. The Mass is, in this sense, the rite of the individuation process. The humanity of Christ symbolizes the ego; his divinity, the unconscious. The Mass therefore expresses symbolically the union of the conscious and the unconscious in the process of individuation.

In archaic men and women the numinous experience of the individuation process was the prerogative of shamans and medicine men; they experienced sickness, torture, and regeneration. These experiences in the Christian person, at a higher level, for Jung, imply the idea of being made whole through sacrifice, of being changed by transubstantiation and exalted to the pneumatic person --- in a world, of apotheosis. The Mass is the summation of a development which began many thousands of years ago.

Jung, by uncovering the unconscious archetypes of religious dogmas, enables us to recognize anthropomorphic elements in our expression and our understanding of those dogmas and simultaneously, to acknowledge in gratitude God's having fitted the glass of revelation to the dark eye of the unconscious as well as to the clearer sight of the mind. To a remarkable extent revelation itself may be seen as a divine adjustment to a kind of reality, the human reality of the unconscious.

As Louis Beirnaert remarks, "It is through the mediation of myths that the salvation inaugurated in the fine point of the soul penetrated to the depths of the psyche. The revival by Christ and by the Church of the great images such as the sun, the moon, the wood, water, mother, etc., signifies an evangelization of the affective powers designated by the images. God has intervened even in the collective unconscious in order to save it and to fulfill it (259).

Jung sees the particular kind of symbol that is known as a dogma as having a twofold positive value. On the one hand it is a substitute for being confronted with the unconscious with an intermediary --- and experience proves that such a confrontation overtakes most people's psychic strength and is always fraught with peril. On the other hand it does justice to the unconscious components of psychic life, even though it does so in the form of a projection (260).

It is the relationship between dogmas and the needs of the human psyche discovered empirically which makes Jung's ideas of dogmas valuable. There is in the person a religious instinct endowed with energy which finds its natural object in dogmas, especially Christian dogmas. In other words, aside from the truths about God that dogmas contain, dogmas fulfill a collective and individual psychological function related to the unconscious needs of our psyche. There is a true psychological affinity between the needs of the unconscious and the gods formulated in dogmas.

What depth psychology has discovered about the laws of growth as they have been known on the spiritual plane. Of course, the idea that the supernatural is analogous to the natural is not new. If God wanted to communicate with us, it is reasonable to think that He would choose those channels which are most intimate to us, that He would bend down to reach us at the simplest yet deepest level.

Of course, as we have explained all along, Catholicism accepts the reality of both natural and supernatural theology. How the two are delineated and distinguished is a complex process, reflecting the complexity of the human person in his attachments to both the natural and the supernatural. Often, for instance, people may believe that the higher power is supernaturally located because of their inability to find it within human experience. The circumstance that people do not know that the higher power is inside their experience does not mean that their experience does not contain it, since the differentiation of components of the interior life is not an easy, clear process.

A major thesis of Jungian analysis is that vital psychic factors are found in interior experience as unconscious contents. Only if such factors become lifted from ordinary experience by means of symbolic images or else fully differentiated by intellectual analysis do people become aware of their existence. A typical task of Jungian psychology is to disclose to the individual what his interior experience contains. This interior experience is dim and evanescent at best, so the demonstration does not proceed with the facile obviousness of disclosing objects which perceptual experience of the interior world contains.

When the concept of the "unconscious" and the concept of the "supernatural" are examined, they are found to mean something which the individual is unable to find in experience, at least under ordinary circumstances. only individual meet his God face to face. This can more regularly be duplicated by the individual achieving spiritual insight through orderly processes of study and personality development.

Ultimately, Catholicism suggests the kind of synthesis that Jung so hungrily sought in the world of religion. The synthesis, or middle way, is to be found in the incorporation of both the natural and the supernatural in its systematic structure. Grace builds upon nature.

The inclusion of both worshipper and God in the field of the personality system unquestionably comes as a serious difficulty to those schooled in traditional Christianity with its sharp separation between the person and God. At the opposite extreme are the traditional Eastern religions who hold the idea that the supreme object of religious devotion is part of one system with human personality, or stated alternatively, human selves are part of the larger self, God. That the higher power of religion is within, not outside of human life and experience, is strongly asserted in Buddhism and Taoism.

While the irrational dimension of the person cannot be dismissed from an analysis of his behavior, Catholicism still believes that rationality is the primary constituent in defining the human person and that it must be given more prominent consideration than Jung gives it in his writings.

Yet it is becoming clearer that the revelatory process consists not of propositional communication, not of words uttered by deity and heard and recorded by us, but rather of the occurrence of images in the mind of men and women. These images, luminous, powerful and sacred, are the medium of God's self-manifestation to us.

To the extent that a sacramentalism neglects to make use of archetypal figures, and reduces its ritual to a schematic unfolding,

it loses its efficacy over the pagan which slumbers in each of us ---
it fails to evangelize the depths. That is when the archetypes which
are themselves idols cause paganism to rise again. It is then too
that one is tempted to turn away from Christianity to seek in other
figures and in other numinous symbolizations the peace of the
depths.

The immense interest presented today by the study of the Fathers
and of ritual originates in part in the need to discover a Christianity
which knew how to address itself effectively to the unconscious of
the natural religious person. The symbolic categories of the
Fathers, Jung has aptly remarked, are those which depth
psychology has disclosed in the structure of the psyche. They are
archetypal. One understands nothing of their thought without
apprehending for example the presence and the activity of the
mother, in the unity which they discover amid the primordial earth
whence was drawn Adam, Eve, the Virgin Mary, baptismal water,
the Church, etc.

It is in part because contemporary Christianity has not known how
to recognize the immanent as well as the transcendent value of the
great symbols which abound in its traditions and in its rituals that
the contemporary psyche has been prey to so many demons, and
finds itself tempted to seek nourishing typologies elsewhere. The
need is not for the theologian to renounce the affirmations of faith,
but to explore a too-neglected dimension of religious symbolism

and on this point to accept the assistance of mythologists and psychologists. It is such an assistance that Carl Jung offers to Catholicism.

Jung never intended that his psychological analysis of the person should replace that of theology. Rather, psychology was meant to help the person understand and appreciate what is the object of theology --- God and the human person insofar as he relates to God. Though this paper has pointed out some of the problems of Jung in relation to magisterial thinking, there is a considerable contribution that Jung can make to theological formulation.

Ultimately, Jung and Catholicism are in agreement that 'God' is a mystery that cannot be unveiled (261). And no theologian could better say that what Jung himself has remarked:

> No matter what the world thinks about religious experience, the one who has it possesses a great treasure, a thing that has become for him a source of life, meaning and beauty, and that has given a new splendor to the world and to mankind. He has pistis and peace. (262).

Endnotes

1. Christianity prides itself upon being a "revealed" religion. And however Catholics may otherwise understand the nature of "revelation" there is no major disagreement on at least this point: Christianity derives its "salvific" efficacy, its essential truth, its value and validity as religion, not from the effectiveness of human understanding but from the self-communication of God.

2. "Catholic theology" will be explained in subsequent pages.

3. From the traditional Catholic theology according to which "grace perfects nature," and sin, while it disintegrates, does not destroy the inherent goodness of human nature, we may reasonably look for some more positive and constructive contacts with empirical psychology. For such a theology, divine forgiveness is no mere "imputation," but really healing and integrating on the natural level which comes under psychological scrutiny.

4. The fact is that with the knowledge and actual experience of inner unconscious images a way is opened for reason and feeling to gain access to other images which the teachings of religion offer to mankind. Psychology thus does just the opposite of what it is accused of: it provides possible approaches to a better undertanding of these things, it opens people's eyes to the real meaning of dogmas, and, far from destroying it, it throws open an empty house to new inhabitants." Psychology and Alchemy, p.2.

5. Moral Theology deals with the actions of the human person. In the last two or three centuries our understanding of the human person and the world has dramatically changed. Unfortunately all the changes in this understanding have had little or no effect as yet on Catholic moral theology. See Absolutes in Moral Theology, p. 10.

6. See Sacramentum Mundi, New York: Herder and Herder, 1970, Vol. III, p. 123.

7. Bernard Lonergan observes that Catholic theology usually arrives on the scene a little breathlessly and a little late. Catholic theology in general and moral theology in particular have not kept pace with the revolutions which have characterized the human person's understanding of self and the world in which he or she lives. See Curran's Absolutes in Moral Theology, p. 11.

8. Ever since the Reformation, Roman Catholic life and theology have tended to exist in a ghetto and react defensively to any of the advances of the time. The Reformation, the Enlightenment and scientific advances were looked upon as threats to Catholic belief and teachings. The Catholic Church in general opted for a position of intransigence and opposition to the thinking of the modern world. Absolutes in Moral Theology, Washington D.C.: Corpus Books, 1968, p.14.

9. This substructure consists of "principles" rather than "doctrines" according to a well-known distinction of Newman. They express the general conditions under which the objects of faith are revealed. Although we are sure of them through faith, it is better to say that they are not parts of the object of faith but rather determine the general conditions of the object.

10. Sacramentum Mundi, Vol. VI, p. 235

11. Sacramentum Mundi, Vol. VI, pp. 239-240.

12. See Chapter Four, "Soul and Psyche."

13. Both theology and psychology maintain that men and women should live full lives in which all their capabilities find full expression, that in doing so they should feel that they fit smoothly into their physical and social environment, that each should make a full contribution to the good of the whole, that they should be free from frustrations arising from their own inadequacy, and that the life of each should be guided by someone or something which they feel to transcend their own individual being.

14. At least in terms of interpretation of the unconscious strata for conscious activity. As the discussion unfolds, it will be seen that Jung has not dealt comprehensively with areas that others consider imperative to the human situation. Love and community are two examples. But Jung's system prefers other virtues which leave intact his 'systems concept.'

15. Analytical psychology is the name reserved for depth psychology that was developed by Carl Jung.

16. Although it began as part of the protest against religion, the net result of modern psychology has been to reaffirm the person's experience of self as a spiritual being. Despite its conscious intention, the discipline of psychology recalls the modern person to an awareness of inner life, thus re-establishing the ancient religious knowledge that our fundamental accomplishments begin within ourselves.

We are now in the midst of a transformation affecting the fundamental nature and spirit of psychological work. Depth psychology in particular, by which we mean all the varied theories interpreting the "unconscious depths" of the human person has arrived at conclusions that reverse the major assumptions with which psychology began as a field of major study. Its culminating insights suggest not only a new conception of human personality, but a new approach to religions as well as a change in the way we see ourselves in history. See Ira Progoff's The Death and Rebirth of Psychology, New York: McGraw-Hill Book Company, 1973.

17. The four most prolific Catholic commentators on Jung are Victor White, Raymond Hostie, Antonio Moreno and Josef Goldbrunner.

18. C.G. Jung: "Religion is a relationship to the highest or most powerful value, be it positive or negative. The relationship is voluntary as well as involuntary, that is to say you can accept, consciously, the value by which you are possessed unconsciously.

That psychological fact which wields the greatest power in your system functions as a god, since it is always the overwhelming psychic factor that is called god." Psychology and Religion: West and East, p. 81.

19. See, for example, Ernesto Buonaiuti's "The Mystic Vision," Eranos Jahrbuch, Vol. VI, 1970.

20. Modern Man in Search of a Soul, p. 217.

21. "We of today have a psychology founded on experience, and not upon articles of faith. The very fact that we have such a psychology is to me symptomatic of a profound convulsion of spiritual life." Modern Man in Search of a Soul, New York: Harcourt, Brace, and World, 1933, p.202.

22. As one Freudian puts it, "The increasing support given to Jungian psychology by clerics can be regarded less as a tribute to Jung's religiosity than as a reaction to Freud's view that religion is one of the illusions wherein man seeks to soften the asperities of life and to stay the fundamental discontents engendered by civilization. It is all the more necessary therefore to point out what is apparently effectively concealed in a mass of Jungian verbiage, that so far from being religious in tendency, Jung's system is fundamentally irreligious. Nobody is to care whether God exists, Jung least of all. All that is necessary is to 'experience' an 'attitude' because it 'helps one to live.'" See Freud or Jung, p. 149.

23. See "Psychoanalysis and Catholicism," in Cross Currents of Psychiatry and Catholic Morality, p. 67.

24. Jungians argue that present day science is based wholly on causality. But causality is only one principle, and psychology cannot be exhausted by causal methods only, because the mind lives by aims as well.

25. "Everything I have written has a double bottom," Jung once said. So that the reader does find a logically understandable

argument on the one hand, but on the other finds himself at the same time exposed to the impact of the 'other voice,' the unconscious, which may either grip him or frighten him off. That 'other voice' can, among other factors, be heard in Jung's special way of reviving the original etymological meanings of words and of allowing both feeling and imaginative elements to enter into his scientific exposition. See C.G. Jung, His Myth in Our Time, p.4.

26. Crises are a necessary precondition for the emergence of novel theories. Thomas Kuhn develops this idea in his influential book, The Structure of Scientific Revolutions.

27. Probably the single most prevalent claim advanced by the proponents of a new paradigm is that they can solve the problems that have led the old one to a crisis.

28. Jung has been brought to the conclusion that repressed religion is at the root of most of our modern malaise, both in the individual and in society. As he has written, "Whenever the Spirit of God is excluded from human consideration, an unconscious substitution takes its place." Civilization in Transition, p. 83.

29. This is a major theme in Modern Man in Search of a Soul.

30. For Jung, we are moved by the laudable and useful ambition to extirpate the chaos of the irrational both within and without to the best of our ability. Two Essays on Analytical Psychology, CW, Vol. 7, p. 171.

31. This idea is developed by Jung in Civilization in Transition, CW, Vol. 10, p. 92.

32. The unconscious is at best a postulate, known (as is God, according to Aquinas) by its phenomenal effects. It is primarily a negative concept for what is not conscious; and however valuable, and indeed indispensable, it is as a postulate, or working hypothesis, it can positively "explain" precisely nothing at all.

33. The Structure and Dynamics of the Psyche, CW, Vol. 8, p. 108.

34. Jung is never tired of emphasizing that a psychic event is an event; but he does not care to add that a true notion differs from a false notion though both exist as a psychic events. Though all of us are influenced by unconscious material, some are subject to illusory perceptions that lead not to a healthy personality development but to destructive ideas and/or unacceptable behavior.

35. The Structure and Dynamics of the Psyche, p. 109.

36. Jung tells us in The Structure and The Dynamics of the Psyche that "consciousness is primarily an organ of orientation in a world of outer and inner facts. First and foremost it establishes the fact that something is there. I call this faculty sensation. By this I do not mean the specific activity of any one of the senses, but perception in general. Another faculty interprets what is perceived; this I call thinking. By means of this function, the object perceived is assimilated and its transformation into a psychic content proceeds much further than in mere sensation. A third faculty establishes the value of the object. This function of evaluation I call feeling. The pain-pleasure reaction of feeling marks the highest degree of subjectivation of the object. Feeling brings subject and object into such a close relationship that the subject must choose between acceptance and rejection. Intuition is an immediate awareness of the relationships that could not be established by the other three functions at the moment of orientation." p. 123.

37. In the last analysis, psychic life is for the greater part an unconscious life that surrounds consciousness on all sides --- a notion that is sufficiently obvious when one considers how much unconscious preparation is needed, for instance, to register a sense impression.

38. According to Jung, it would never do to foist our conscious psychology upon the unconscious. Its mentality is an instinctive

one; it has no differentiated functions, and it does not "think" as we understand "thinking." It simply creates an image that answers to the conscious situation. This image contains as much thought as feeling, and is anything rather than a product of rationalistic reflection. See Two Essays on Analytical Psychology, p. 182.

39. The individual content of consciousness is the most favorable object imaginable for psychology, precisely because it has differentiated the universal to the point of unrecognizability. The essence of conscious process is adaptation, which takes place in a series of particulars; the unconscious, on the other hand, is universal --- it not only binds individuals together into a nation or race, but unites them with the people of the past and with their psychology. Thus, by reason of its supra-individual universality, the unconscious is the prime object of any real psychology that claims to be more than psychophysics. See Symbols of Transformation, p. 177.

40. Jung distinguishes between archetypes and instincts. These both form part of the human being, but instincts are right at the opposite end of the scale from archetypes. Instincts are an expression of the biological side of human nature, archetypes of the spiritual side. As the two sides together make up the whole range of dispositions, they create a state of conflict which is simply "the expression and perhaps also the foundation, of the tension which we term psychic energy." See Hostie's Religion and the Psychology of Jung, New York: Sheed and Ward, 1957, p. 123.

41. See Jung, God's and Modern Man, South Bend: University of Notre Dame Press, 1970, p. 60.

42. Laurens Van der Post says that "Victor White was to turn on Jung with, it seems to me, unnecessary violence and reprehensible disregard of what he owed him both as teacher and friend." See Jung and the Story of our Time, p. 222.

43. See Soul and Psyche, p. 226.

44. Ibid., Raymond Hostie, p. 63.

45. The usual manifestation of the archetypes occurs when man is placed in special psychological states, like dreams, active imagination and schizophrenia. The archetypes reveal themselves as clothed in modern dress and they appear simultaneously with conscious material.

46. Jung believes that we "possess" many things which we have never acquired but have inherited from our ancestors. We are not born as a tabula rasa, we are merely born unconscious. But we bring with us systems that are organized and ready to function in a specifically human way, and these we owe to millions of years of human development. See Freud and Psychoanalysis, p. 315.

47. Readers of Jung have always to be remembering that his use of the word "religion" is equivocal. The religious symbol which as a dogma constitutes the very essence of a creed is in point of fact simply something that comes after a direct personal experience. The genuine religious experience, on the other hand, is simply a direct awareness of the numinous, differing not at all in value from the symbolism of the alchemists, both being made up of projections of the same order. Dogmatic religion and alchemy are not essentially different; they differ only in the specific form of their symbols.

48. The Symbolic Life, p. 723.

49. Jung is, of course, aware that religion can also be considered within a theological and historical frame of reference, and would perhaps even insist that enough has already been said about the institutional needs of the religious group, and that we need to devote our attention and resources to caring for the individual who has become disordered as the result of the pressures from the group.

50. David Cox challenges the transposing of religious, and psychological vocabulary. Christians speak of "salvation," "eternal

Life," "Christlikeness," "obedience to God," and so on; Jung speaks of "individuation," "integration," "accepting the unconscious," "the appearance of a new center," and things like that. He says that no attempt to compare directly ideals set before us in such different languages can possibly result in anything but confusion, and nothing but harm is done by those who unthinkingly compare psychological and religious formulae as though they belonged to a single language. See Jung and St. Paul, p. 4.

51. See The Symbolic Life, p. 736.

52. Aion, part 2, p. 34.

53. Jung asserts that in psychology one possesses nothing unless one has experienced it in reality. Hence a purely intellectual insight is not enough, because one knows only the words and not the substance of a thing from inside. See Aion, part 2, p. 33.

54. Investigation of the products of the unconscious yields recognizable traits of archetypal structures which coincide with myth-motifs, among them certain types which deserve the name of dominants. These are archetypes like the anima, animum, wise old man, witch, shadow, earth-mother, etc., and the quaternity. It is evident that knowledge of these types makes myth interpretation considerably easier and at the same time puts it where it belongs; that is, on a psychic basis. See Symbols of Transformation, p. 390.

55. Aion, part 2, p. 35.

56. Jung develops this idea in Symbols of Transformation, p. 227.

57. As Eliade says, the significance of symbols regarding religion cannot be solved by depth psychology alone, "for the symbolisms which decipher the latter are for the most part made up of scattered fragments and of the manifestations of a psyche in crises, if not in a state of pathological regression. To grasp the authentic structures and functions of symbols, one must turn to the inexhaustible indices of the history of religions; and yet even here, one must

know how to choose." This makes the problem involved and difficult. See Images and Symbols, New York: Sheed and Ward, 1961, p. 37.

58. Jung says, "It is indeed not a God that 'modern consciousness' abhors, but faith. Whatever may be the case concerning God, the important thing for the man of modern consciousness is to stand in no further relation of faith to Him." See The Eclipse of God, p. 114.

59. See Freud and Psychoanalysis, p. 193.

60. See Symbols of Transformation, p. 229.

61. Jung realized that Christianity has played a positive part in human history. But he wanted it to be a part that came to an end, because he thought it was a source of error. He demanded, or rather desired, that the age of symbolic illusion should give place to an age of moral autonomy. See Hostie's Religion and the Psychology of Jung, New York: Sheed and Ward, 1957, p. 120.

62. Freud and Psychoanalysis, p. 335.

63. R. Hostie and Victor White both agree that from the Catholic position Jung does not show much sign of fitting into "Roman philosophy." Though Hostie consistently accepts Jung as a scientist, he discredits him as a theologian.

64. For Jung, the God-image is not something invented, it is an experience that comes upon man spontaneously.

65. See Jung, Gods, and Modern Man, p. 253.

66. Nature is conservative and does not easily allow her courses to be altered. Jung maintains this position through all of his writings.

67. Of course, this is violently disputed.

68. See "Faith and Psyche; A Role for Jung in Theology", p. 172.

69. See The Objective Psyche, p. 129.

70. I have not come across anything in Jung's writings to substantiate this statement. Johnson himself does not document it.

71. "One cannot grasp anything metaphysically, one only can do so psychologically. Therefore I strip things of their metaphysical wrappings in order to make them objects of psychology. In that way I can at least extract something understandable from them and avail myself of it, and I also discover psychological facts and processes that before were veiled in symbols and beyond my comprehension. In doing so I may perhaps be following in the footsteps of the faith, and may possibly have similar experiences; and if in the end there should be something ineffably metaphysical behind it all, it would then have the best opportunity of showing itself." See Alchemical Studies, p. 49.

72. Jung's conception of creation has little in common with that of most Christians. For him, creation implies the acquisition of consciousness of the universe, especially of the human person. Why? Because the purpose of creation is connected with the transformation of God; the encounter with the creature changes the Creator. The purpose of creation is the necessity of a greater consciousness in God. This is the message Jung gets from the biblical Job.

73. Buber is illustrative of those, Christian and non-Christian alike, who do not accept the Jungian point of view that in religious matters we deal more with the 'inside' than the 'outside.'

74. Transcendence refers to the transformation the sovereign and eternal God has effected upon the concrete human situation in terms of reconciliation, redemption, the restoration of health, the amelioration of social and political divisions, and so on. Transcendence must be grasped, not as it has so often been in the past, in spatial terms, referring to the God up there, beyond the

affairs of human life, but specifically in terms of what God has effected historically on behalf of the human person.

75. This is the Buber argument outlined in Eclipse of God.

76. See "Carl Jung, Psychology and Catholicism," p. 315.

77. See The Idea of the Holy, London: Oxford University Press, 1943.

78. Ibid, p. 106.

79. Ibid, p. 275.

80. "Mysterium Conjunctionis," in the Catholic Educational Review, p. 275.

81. Karl Stern writes that hardly anything has even been said about the neurosis of unbelief. "This is not surprising, since to most investigators, faith ('the certainty of things we have not seen') is an abnormal or at least a suspect phenomenon. In my own experience, lack of religious faith or loss of faith has often proved to be a serious indication of a disordered person." See The Third Revolution, New York: Harcourt, Brace and Company, 1954, p. 283.

82. Louis Beirnaert supports Meier's view: "There are men with deformed psychic structures who, poor in natural dispositions for a life conformed to the moral law, will never be virtuous and who will stumble from weakness to weakness to the very end of their lives. There are some whose psychic structures render them arid and make of them incurable rationalizers. They will never have any relish for the sacraments and for simply submission to mystery. There are men with infantile psychic structures, haunted by a hunger for security, obsessed by a false sense of guilt, and possessed of so many shortcomings great and small, that they will probably never experience lucidity in their value judgments and constancy in acts formed by the will. Are all these --- and they are

innumerable --- really unsuited for sanctification?" See <u>Cross Currents of Psychiatry and Catholic Morality</u>, p. 145.

83. See <u>Ancient Incubation and Modern Psychotherapy</u>, Evanston: Northwestern University Press, 1967, P. 124.

84. See <u>Psychological Types</u>, p. 41.

85. <u>Freud and Psychoanalysis</u>, p. 334.

86. An argument that Victor White regularly brings up in his writings.

87. See <u>The Practice of Psychotherapy</u>, p. 79.

88. See <u>Existential Psychology</u>, New York: Herder and Herder, 1964, p. IX.

89. There are those who consider it best to unmask Jung as an "unconscious believer" who, while claiming to be no more than a psychologist, has tried to do again what the gnostics tried to do so presumptuously in the past.

90. See David Tracey's <u>Blessed Rage for Order</u>.

91. See Macquarrie's <u>Principles of Christian Theology</u>.

92. <u>The Symbolic Life</u>, p. 127.

93. These ideas are examined in Ward's <u>The Concept of God</u>, New York: St. Martin's Press, 1974.

94. <u>The Symbolic Life</u>, p. 127.

95. Philosophy is generally held to have truth as its subject, while cosmology examines the world.

96. See <u>The Strucutre and Dynamics of the Psyche</u>, p. 343.

97. See Denzinger's Enchiridion Symbolorum Definitionum ed Declarationum, number 1670.

98. Ibid, number 2192.

99. Some theologians teach that the human person in a "natural" state is evil, burdened by original sin. On the other hand, Jung finds in the unconscious material of his patients evidences of the highest spiritual potentiality as well as the possibility of deepest degradation.

100. Here is a good example of different meanings being attached to the same word. The Vatican Council was speaking out of the Greek epistemological schema whereby the rational inductive-deductive process leads to a specific object; in this case, God. Jung dispenses with such a formal rational process. For him, God is an overwhelming psychic experience.

101. When Jung speaks of knowing God, he is referring to the experiential knowledge which is not dissimilar to the knowledge of natural theology.

102. See Goldbrunner's Individuation, p. 159.

103. The Secret of the Golden Flower, London: Routledge, 1931.

104. The question of the boundaries of the psyche comes to its sharpest focus when we consider God in relation to the psyche. In the vastness of this field that includes our conscious and unconscious, Jung saw God at work. So when Jung calls God an autonomous factor in the pscyhe, he does not mean that God is something to be found only within ourselves.

105. Ibid., p. 267.

106. Jung constantly says that he has never anywhere denied God.

107. "There is no one thing, no one single event, called revelation; there are countless revelations of varying kinds and very varying degrees. The task of theology is not to lay down some a priori pattern of how God should reveal and what he should reveal; its task to bow down in deep humility before the manifold and bewildering variety of what God actually does; to accept it, in the first place, as naked, unchangeable fact, however offensive or otherwise it may be to particular human tastes and preconceptions." Victor White, God and the Unconscious, p. 112.

108. Psychology and Religion, West and East, p. 74.

109. Some authors argue that what Jung and Otto call religion, that which they honestly believe to be religion, that which they honestly believe to be religion, is not religion at all, even from the empirical point of view. For them, it appears to be only a very incidental manifestation. This position is taken by A. Leonard (La Vie Spirituelle) and many others.

110. Rudolf Otto The Idea of the Holy (Oxford, 1943), p. 12. Quoted in Jung's Psychology and Religion, p. 7.

111. This list originates in Buber's Eclipse of God. Chapters five, "Religion and Modern Thinking," and seven, "Reply to C.G. Jung," contain valuable material.

112. See Buber's Eclipse of God, p. 78.

113. Ibid, p. 81.

114. Ibid,, pp. 90-91.

115. Ibid., pp. 87-90.

116. See Buber's Eclipse of God, p. 79.

117. See Buber's Eclipse of God, p. 81.

118. Ibid., pp. 133-137.

119. Denzinger, 2072.

120. Without necessity, nothing in human nature bridges, the human personality least of all. It is tremendously conservative , not to say torpid. Only acute necessity is able to rouse it. Jung takes this view in The Development of Personality, p. 173. His writings never deviate from it.

121. This issue can be seen in the chapter dealing with the theologian's 'soul' and the psychologist's 'psyche.'

122. See Victor White's God the Unknown, p. 68.

123. Faith, Reason and Modern Psychiatry, New York: P.J. Kenedy & Sons, 1955.

124. The value of the symbol does not depend merely on historical causes; its chief importance lies in the fact that it has a meaning for the actual present and for the future, in their psychological aspects. For the Jungian School the symbol is not merely a sign of something repressed and concealed, but is at the same time an attempt to comprehend and to point the way to the further psychological development of the individual.

125. Analysis and reduction lead to causal truth; this by itself does not help us to live but only induces resignation and hopelessness. On the other hand, the recognition of the intrinsic value of a symbol leads to constructive truth and helps us to live; it inspires hopefulness and furthers the possibility of future development.

126. See Jung's "Letter to Upton Sinclair," New Republic, 1955.

127. See Religion, Language and Truth, New York: Herder and Herder, 1970, p. 293.

128. See Dewart's Religion, Language and Truth.

129. This enigma is spelled out in Sacramentum Mundi's treatment of the subject in Vol. II, p. 307.

130. Salvation is the 'making whole' of human existence. Though subject to many biblical and theological perspectives, salvation, in the fullest Christian sense, means the healing of the ills of humanity, and the imparting of light and life. Such salvation is the fruit of the whole incarnate life of Jesus Christ, including His death and resurrection. For an extensive explanation of "salvation," see Sacramentum Mundi, Vol V.

131. These four meanings are developed in Jean Moroux' The Christian Experience. New York: Sheed and Ward, 1954.

132. Reality as that which actually exists; that which is not imagination, fiction, or pretense. Not merely an idea, it is something neither derivative nor dependent.

133. Jung tells us that "constructive understanding differs from scholastic speculation in that it never asserts that something has universal validity, but merely subjective validity. When a speculative philosopher believes he has comprehended the world once and for all in his systems, he is deceiving himself; he has merely comprehended himself and then naively projected that view upon the world. Projection is a fundamental error of scholasticism that has lingered on into modern times. Reacting against this, 'scientism' almost put an end to speculation and went to the other extreme. It tried to create an 'objective' psychology. In the face of these efforts, the emphasis that Freud laid on the psychology of the individual is of immortal merit. The immense importance of subjective factors in the development of objective mental processes was thus given due prominence for the first time." See The Psychogenesis of Mental Disease, p. 185.

134. At the turn of the century, James and Henri Bergson were already objecting to the prevailing tendency in Western rationalism to limit knowledge to mere cognitive abstraction capable of

prediction and control but incapable of understanding. Now the therapeutic disciplines have demonstrated that reflection is, indeed, transformative when personal knowledge is integrally related to experience. The person is changed by what he knows when his knowing remains rooted in existential realities --- where the ambiguities of pain and joy, anxiety and hope, are mediated through interpersonal experience, symbol, and dramatic reenactment.

135. See Two Essays on Analytical Psychology, p. 124.

136. This idea is discussed in Vol. V of Sacramentum Mundi, p. 292.

137. According to some writers, Jung stresses experience, as against Christianity which stresses the intellectual surrender even against our own feelings, as happens in periods of aridity and especially in the mystic purification of faith --- the dark night of the soul. But, although faith in itself depends essentially on the intellect and will --- the two spiritual powers --- it is also true that it is the person who believes, the whole person, and feelings and human experiences undoubtedly help the assent of the act of faith, especially in the first stages of Christian life.

138. There seems to be no statistical evidence whatever that the incidence of immediate, individual experience (however this may be defined) is any lower among Catholics or Evangelicals than anybody else; indeed there is evidence that among many of them such experiences are both rich and frequent.

139. Creeds and doctrines just as easily expose a believer to immediate experience as to shield him from it. The original revelational experiences are shared in every time and place with the whole Church, whose very foundations rest upon the experiences of the prophets and apostles. The communication and re-living of these original experiences belongs to the Church's very raison d'etre. And they are shared, first and foremost, not by the

imparting of conceptual information from outside, but by the direct sensory and imaginative processes of the recipients.

140. To a practicing Catholic, the doctrine of transubstantiation is not an intellectual theory with no relation to his experience; it is a statement about the facts of his familiar experience in attending Mass and receiving Communion. The crucifix is a familiar fact to him before he learns any conceptualized doctrine of the atonement, and when he does learn such a doctrine, it is meaningful only in relation to that experienced fact.

141. See Denzinger's Enchiridion, no. 2081.

142. According to Catholic teaching, the God dimension of the faith equation remains constant while the human dimension constantly changes.

143. The assumption that Catholics share a single or unified perception of God's being may not stand up under examination. Though they start from a common revelation, the perceptions of God are, as I point out elsewhere, legion.

144. See Ward's The Concept of God, p. 168.

145. See Denzinger, no. 1789.

146. Of course not everyone would concur in this view. Dewart promotes it in Religion, Language and Truth. He gets a mixed reaction from both philosophers and theologians.

147. See Jung's Psychology and Religion, p. 108.

148. Altizer observes that Jung's work has theological value only insofar as he succeeded in creating a peculiarly modern form of Gnosticism. Like all forms of gnosis, it is grounded in a nondialectical negationof the world finally dissolving reason, consciousness, and history in its search for a total consummation

and liberation of the "self." See <u>Mircea Eliade and the Dialectic of the Sacred</u>, Philadelphia: The Westminster Press, 1963.

149. See <u>Principles of Christian Theology</u>, New York: Charles Scribner's Sons, 1966, pp. 59-64.

150. See <u>Psychology and Religion: West and East</u>, p. 360.

151. An assertion Jung makes in <u>Psychology and Alchemy</u>, p. 15.

152. <u>Civilization in Transition</u>, p. 256.

153. <u>Psychological Types</u>, p. 454.

154. <u>Civilization in Transition</u>, p. 293.

155. <u>Psychology and Religion: West and East</u>, pp. 331-332.

156. <u>The Psychogenesis of Mental Disease</u>, p. 193.

157. Unless we accept a psychic version of the chicken and the egg controversy, and argue that the wheel and the door were psychic phenomena before they were physical ones.

158. See Philipson's <u>Outline of a Jungian Aesthetics</u>, Evanston: Northwestern University Press, 1963, p. 141.

159. David Tracy lists that along with Christian texts. See <u>Blessed Rage for Order</u>, p. 43.

160. Jolande Jacobi's <u>The Way of Individuation</u>, New York: Harcourt, Brace and World, 1967, p. 98.

161. <u>The Way of Individuation</u>, p. 79.

162. The discussion of analogy is a common feature of theological manuals that rely on scholastic philosophy. As an example, see Ott's <u>Fundamentals of Catholic Dogma</u>, p. 19.

163. This idea is developed in Benson's <u>Religion in Contemporary Culture</u>, p. 268.

164. <u>Psychology and Religion: West and East</u>, p. 303.

165. This explains how it is possible to re-live the immanent divine life in the actuality of the true self, as in Eckhart's <u>scintilla animae</u>. See <u>Sacramentum Mundi</u>, Vol. 6, pp. 138-40.

166. A general description of the soul can be obtained from various sources. The one depicted here draws upon Bouyer's <u>Dictionary of Theology</u>, New York: Desclee and Company, 1965.

167. See <u>Sacramentum Mundi</u>, Vol. VI, p. 140.

168. L'Osservatore Romano, Giovedi 16 Aprile, 1953, p. 1.

169. See Ott, p. 102.

170. See <u>Psychological Types</u>, p. 250.

171. The soul, says Jung, must contain in itself the faculty of relation to God, i.e., a correspondence, and this correspondence is, in psychological terms, the archetypes of the God-image. What is therefore God? The soul's deepest and closest intimacies is precisely what God is. If God lies in the deepest and closest intimacies of the soul, his properties will reflect --- at least psychologically speaking --- the properties of the unconscious where he lies. The properties of God have to be imbued with anthropomorphic traits, the qualities of the unconscious. For instance, since man is continuously evolving, God is also evolving and appears in different ways. As Jolande Jacobi says, "The metamorphosis of the gods in our outward and inward worlds is inexhaustible, and never closes." <u>(Complex, Archetype, Symbol in the Psychology of C.G. Jung)</u>.

172. See <u>The Practice of Psychotherapy</u>.

173. There is a tendency among laymen in psychology to think of the psyche as contained only within the four walls of the body, i.e., the psyche is inside of me, even less than the whole of me. Such is not Jung's view. For him the psyche might be considered the field of all things known and unknown, the pivot of the world. It cannot be said to be only inside of us. If, sitting in the chair where you now are, you not only can think of some loved one across the sea but can, under certain circumstances, project yourself into his presence in such a way as to have an effect upon him, you cannot say that the psyche is something existing only inside of you.

174. See The Structure and Dynamics of the Psyche, p. 139.

175. Many hold a different view, namely, that psychology is still simply a part of philosophy. As part of that they maintain that for thousands of years psychology was a branch of philosophy. The subject of psychology, the study of the person, was subordinate to the total world view, that is to a hierarchy in which God, the world and all it contains, and the person with his own characteristics, feelings and thoughts, had not yet been wrenched apart but formed a coherent whole.

176. See The Structure and Dynamics of the Psyche, p. 276.

177. Jung's conclusions about the religious side of the psyche: 1) A spiritual element is an organic part of the human psyche; 2) Such elements are regularly expressed in symbols; 3) These symbols reveal a path of psychological development which can be traced, not only backward toward a cause in the past, but forward toward a goal in the future; 4) The goal is expressed by images of completion in a whole which calls the Self and which is unique for each individual. It is formed by the integration of the little self, or ego, and the unconscious; 5) This whole is characterized by all the qualities of numinousness, unconditional authority, power and value which also belong to the image of God.

178. See The Structure and Dynamics of the psyche, p. 278.

179. See <u>Symbols of Transformation</u>, p. 231.

180. The soul is a major part of the psyche. The two words are not interchangeable in Jungian terms because the psyche is more than the soul.

181. <u>Denzinger</u>, no. 2085.

182. <u>Ibid.</u>, no 2087.

183. Hostie's <u>Religion and the Psychology of Jung</u>, p. 13.

184. <u>Psychology and Alchemy</u>, p. 13.

185. <u>Ibid</u>, p. 13.

186. <u>Individuation</u>, p. 189.

187. Nowhere in the Jungian vocabulary do we find a word whose meaning parallels its Christian counterpart as close as does the concept of soul. For Jung, the soul is a major facet of the psyche and it performs many of the functions attributed to the Christian soul. However, Jung takes other functions Christians attribute to the soul and relegates them to the psyche.

188. See <u>Soul and the Psyche</u>, p. 168.

189. <u>Modern Man in Search of a Soul</u>, p. 264.

190. <u>Psychology and Alchemy</u>, p. 11.

191. <u>Freud and Psychoanalysis</u>, p. 764.

192. See <u>Cross Currents of Psychiatry and Catholic Morality</u>, p. 29.

193. Theologians constantly attack Jung for the 'pragmatism' he sees in theological symbols and ideas. See Cattell's Psychology and the Religious Quest, p. 59.

194. See "Social Values and Psychotherapy," Journal of Personality, XIV, pp. 199-228.

195. See Johnson's The Search for Transcendence, p. 113.

196. Contrast this to Goldbrunner: The goal of individuation is the "enthronement of the self" in the clear light of the supra-conscious. Four stages are involved: 1) I; 2) Thou; 3) We; 4) God. These are the four typical problems which life sets every man: 1) authenticity of personal character; 2) sex; 3) community; 4) religion. Dealing with them requires the employment of the conscious and unconscious spiritual energies which might be called the main organs of the human psyche and which must be shaped in a personal mold. Cure of Mind and Cure of Soul, p. 40.

197. See Modern Man in Search of a Soul, p. 263.

198. People who judge Jung by his theoretical attitude will more readily agree with him. People who concentrate on his practical applications or his explicit or implicit conclusions will break with him or launch into violent criticism of him.

199. Jacobi's The Psychology of C.G. Jung, p. 3

200. Jung: "For my part, I prefer to look at man in the light of what in him is healthy and sound and to free the sick man from just that kind of psychology which colors every page Freud has written. I cannot see how Freud can ever get beyond his own psychology and relieve the patient of a suffering from which the doctor himself still suffers." Freud and Psychoanalysis, p. 335.

201. Life itself "analyses" man, which is why it has been suggested that life itself should be termed, somewhat bombastically, the "eternal analysis." Only death brings it to an

end. Death is the final archetype. Those who have survived an otherwise fatal situation have often felt that the experience was an enrichment.

202. See Jung's Integration of the Personality, p. 287.

203. In his theoretical concepts Jung simply does not deal with the problems of interpersonal relations. For him, it goes without saying that everything that happens in the human psyche is the result of a process of growth that comes from within, without there being any need to attach much importance to interaction with the outside world.

204. Psychological Types, p. 563.

205. See Jacobi's The Psychology of Carl Gustav Jung, p. 140.

206. It is required that consciousness should in its own way take an active part in the "marriage" with the contents of the unconscious. Is there a third element which is situated neither in consciousness nor the unconscious but stands above the parties and on which true leadership devolves? The psychotherapist's whole effort must be concentrated on wooing and alluring this third element until it is born and becomes the clear center of the soul. This polarity requires a third force which stands above the opposite poles and embraces them both.

207. p. 52 ff.

208. See The Practice of Psychotherapy, p. 46.

209. This process is described in Two Essays on Analytical Psychology, pp. 290 ff.

210. As Eliade says, "Symbols cannot be reflections of cosmic rhythms as natural phenomena, for a symbol always reveals something more than the aspect of cosmic life it is thought to represent." (Images and Symbols, p. 176). The symbols arise,

from the beginning, as a creation of the unconscious psyche, not as a reflection of a cosmic event.

211. "Rebirth is an affirmation that must be counted among the primordial affirmations of mankind. These primordial affirmations are based on what I call archetypes. In view of the fact that all affirmations relating to the sphere of the supre-sensual are, in the last analysis, invariably determined by archetypes, it is not surprising that a concurrence of affirmations concerning rebirth can be found among the most widely differing peoples. There must be psychic events underlying these affirmations which it is the business of psychology to discuss--without entering into all the metaphysical and philosophical assumptions regarding their significance." (The Archetypes and the Collective Unconscious, p. 116).

212. Psychic evil is to be defined as anything that hinders, prevents, falsifies, or distorts individuation.

213. Joseph L. Henderson says, "Jung rescues religion from dogma; he shows me how to withdraw the mistaken projection." In the end Jung gets rid of any external connotation. Although the withdrawal of the projection is dangerous and is recommended only for a few and just at the end of the process of individuation. Otherwise the withdrawal would entail the danger of inflation, the feeling of God-almightiness.

214. The first condition for moral health is humility; recognition of the shadow is a reason for it, for genuine fear of the abysmal depths of man. This recognition is important because our dark side is not harmless; it brings the archaic psyche, the whole world of archetypes, into direct contact with the conscious world and mind. Consequently, it is imperative to discover our shadow, because insofar as it is conscious there is always a possibility of correction; if repressed, there is no possibility at all, and, on the contrary, it is liable to burst forth suddenly in a moment of awareness, upsetting the ego and breeding neurosis.

215. See Jacobi's The Way of Individuation, p. 34.

216. The Archetypes and the Collective Unconscious, p. 289.

217. See Psychology and Religion, pp. 147 ff.

218. As explained in Aion, p. 45.

219. "The Psychiatrist knows only too well what happens when the two psychic halves, the conscious and the unconscious, split. He knows it as dissociation of the personality; the root of all neuroses: the conscious goes to the right and the unconscious to the left. As opposites never unite at their own level, a supraordinate "third" is always required, in which the two parts can come together.   And since the symbol derives as much from the conscious as from the unconscious, it is able to unite them both, reconciling their conceptual polarity through its form and their emotional polarity through its numinosity." Aion, part 2, p. 180.

220. See Two Essays on Analytical Psychology, p. 19.

221. The material of neurosis, Jung insists, is always understandable in human terms and is related to the personal life of the neurotic; neurosis presupposes individual fantasies, not a loss of reality. But the material appearing in psychosis is not understandable in personal terms; schizophrenia implies a loss of reality and a reactivation of archaic fantasies and thinking that cannot be derived from the conscious mind.

222. See Alchemical Studies, p. 15.

223. Ibid., pp. 45-46.

224. Dogma, says Jung, expresses an irrational whole by means of imagery and reflects the spontaneous and autonomous activity of the objective psyche, the unconscious. Dogmas are not only expressions of the contents of the archetypes, but also of their dynamic autonomous activity; they symbolize the motions of the

libido. Dogmas are imbued with emotional values and express the soul more completely than scientific theories because they last for centuries, as against the dialectical nature of scientific theories. See Moreno's <u>Jung, Gods, and Modern Man</u>, p. 76.

225. Jung made an enthusiastic search for any representations that emphasized the reality of evil. In this connection he has a special liking for the books of the Bible, and even more for the apocryphal writings that concentrate on the conflict between Satan and Christ. He believed that the oldest and truest view of this is to be found where Satan is presented as a "Son" of God, or, to be more precise, as his eldest son, expressing part of his nature --- his "shadow" --- because this brings out the reality of evil and at the same time the fact that it is complementary to good. Jung in fact believes that both good and evil must be present in God.

226. In Jung's view, evil, which is a debilitating psychic force, does not originate from any ontological duality, for it is relative in its origin and ends by leading to a greater good. Evil comes from a false or unsatisfactory attitude, and disappears as soon as this has been corrected. In all human development evil is the way to good.

227. See <u>Aion</u>, p. 50.

228. The transcendent function does not proceed without aim and purpose, but leads to the revelation of the essential man. It is in the first place a purely natural process, which may in some cases pursue its course without the knowledge or assistance of the individual, and can sometimes forcibly accomplish itself in the face of opposition. See Hostie's <u>Religion and the Psychology of Jung</u>, p. 145.

229. See <u>Aion</u>, p. 37.

230. This is developed extensively in Henry's <u>Man and His Happiness</u>, Vol. III.

231.   Etymologically, perfect stems from the Latin perficere (finish, do through to the end) and means "completely done." This is remarkably close to the idea of "wholeness."

232.   Taking advantage of the fantastic and fabulous character of myths in general, theologians customarily point out that Christian dogma contains an essential reference to real history. Thus, insofar as i does relate to historical facts, the Christian faith would cease to be myth. This viewpoint overlooks two points; 1) many myths outside Christianity also rest on some solid historical support and 2) in its dogma the real history of Christianity is a mythified history that has been poetically shaped by faith. On that front, then, the difference between Christian history as evoked by dogma and myths with some historical base is greatly diminished.

233.   The Symbolic Life, p. 669.

234.   See Denzinger, 93, 203, 223, 271.

235.   Developed by Jung in Psychological Types, pp. 13 ff.

236.   See Denzinger, nos. 501-529.

237.   See the introduction to The Secret of the Golden Flower.

238.   See Goldbrunner's Individuation, pp. 154-55.

239.   For Jung, the dogmatically formulated truths of the Christian Church express, almost perfectly, the nature of psychic experience. They are the repositories of the secrets of the soul, and this matchless knowledge is set forth in grand symbolical images. The unconscious thus possesses a natural affinity with the spiritual values of the Church, particularly in their dogmatic form, which owes its special character to centuries of theological controversy --- absurd as this seemed in the eyes of later generations --- and to the passionate efforts of many great men.

240. In any religious discipline it is of the highest importance that one should remain conscious of one's difficulties --- in other words, of one's sins. An excellent means to this end is the mutual confession of sin, which effectively prevents one from becoming unconscious. These measures aim at keeping the conflicts conscious, and that is also a sine qua non of the psychotherapeutic process. The Practice of Psychotherapy, p. 55.

241. See Jung and St. Paul, p. 244.

242. Psychological Types, p. 265.

243. Secret of the Golden Flower, p. 129.

244. See Two Essays on Analytical Psychology, p. 205.

245. Homan's The Dialogue Between Theology and Psychology, Chicago: University of Chicago Press, 1968, p. 2.

246. The Secret of the Golden Flower, p. 129.

247. A letter of 13 March 1958. Taken from Jaffe's Word and Image, p. 207.

248. Memories, Dreams, Reflections, New York: Vintage Books, 1965, p. 210.

249. See Sacramentum Mundi, Vol. VI, pp. 275-281 for the many possible meanings of transcendence.

250. Aion, p. 6.

251. Dogma helps to constitute the unity of faith and makes it visible. Consequently, when it is determined and proclaimed, there always occur not only a manifestation of the reality to which it refers, but also a terminological determination of common linguistic usage. The definition of a dogma often consists just as

much in fixing the common mode of expression as in distinguishing between true and false propositions.

252. See Aion, p. 12.

253. See Jung and the Story of our Time, pp. 104 ff.

254. See Mircea Eliade's The Sacred and the Profane, p. 213.

255. Symbols of Transformation, p. 77.

256. Developed by Jung in Psychology and Religion: West and East, pp. 35 ff.

257. The 1950 definition of Mary's Assumption into heaven.

258. Schaer's Religion and the Cure of Souls in Jung's Psychology, p. 71.

259. See Cross Currents of Psychiatry and Catholic Morality, p. 4.

260. To attain full individuation in the Jungian sense it is necessary to withdraw the external projection which dogmas presuppose: "Individuation can only happen when you withdraw your projections from the outward historical or metaphysical Christ and thus wake up Christ within. The Self (or Christ) cannot become conscious and real without the withdrawal of external projections." See Chapter V, "Christ, A symbol of the Self," in Aion, Part 2.

261. Letter, 23 May 1955, Jaffe's Word and Image, p. 209.

262. Psychology and Religion: West and East, p. 167.

Chapter VI: Bibliography

A. Primary Sources

Clarkson, John, et. al., The Church Teaches, Rockford, Illinois: Tan Books and Publishers, 1973.

Denzinger, Henricus and Adolfus Schoenmetzer, Enchiridion Symbolorum Definitionum et Declarationum, Freiburg: Verlag herder KG, 1963.

Fremantle, Anne, The Papal Encyclicals, New York: new American Library, 1963.

The Freud/Jung Letters, Princeton: Princeton University Press, Bollinger Series XVC, 1973.

Gallagher, Joseph, The Documents of Vatican II, New york: American Press, 1966.

Jung, C.G., Psychiatric Studies, Princeton: Princeton University Press, Volume 1 of the Collected
        Works (CW. 1975).

_____. Experimental Researches, Princeton: Princeton University Press, Volume 2 of the CW,
        1973.

_____. The Psychogenesis of Mental Disease, Princeton: Princeton University Press, Volume 3 of
        the CW, 1972.

_____. Freud and Psychoanalysis, Princeton: Princeton University Press, Volume 4 of the CW,
        1970.

_____. Symbols of Transformation, Princeton: Princeton University Press, Volume 5 of the CW, 1976.

_____. Psychological Types, Princeton: Princeton University Press, Volume 6 of the CW, 1974.

_____. Two Essays on Analytical Psychology, Princeton: Princeton University Press, Volume 7 of the CW, 1975.

_____. The Structure and Dynamics of the Psyche, Princeton: Princeton University Press, Volume 8 of the CW, 1975.

_____. The Archetypes and the Collective Unconscious, Princeton: Princeton University Press, Volume 9 of the CW, Part 1, 1975.

_____. Aion, Princeton: Princeton University Press, Volume 9 of the CW, Part 2, 1975.

_____. Civilization in Transition, Princeton: Princeton University Press, Volume 10 of the CW, 1975.

_____. Psychology and Religion: West and East, Princeton: Princeton University Press, Volume II of the CW, 1975.

_____. Psychology and Alchemy, Princeton: Princeton University Press, Volume 12 of the CW, 1974.

_____. Alchemical Studies, Princeton: Princeton University Press, Volume 13 of the CW, 1976.

_____. Mysterium Conjunctionis, Princeton: Princeton University Press, Volume 14 of the CW,
      1976.

_____. The Spirit in Man, Art and Literature, Princeton: Princeton University Press, Volume 15 of
      the CW, 1975.

_____. The Practice of Psychotherapy, Princeton: Princeton University Press, Volume 16 of the
      CW, 1975.

_____. The Development of Personality, Princeton: Princeton University Press, Volume 17 of the
      CW, 1974.

_____. The Symbolic Life, Princeton: Princeton University Press, Volume 18 of the CW, 1976.

_____. Man and His Symbols, New York: Dell Publishing Co., 1975.

_____. Memories, Dreams, Reflections, New York: Vintage Books, 1965.

_____. Modern Man in Search of a Soul, New York: Harcourt, Brace and World, 1933.

_____. "The Spirit of Psychology," Spirit and Nature, 1955.

Neuner, Josef, and Heinrich Roos, The Teaching of the Catholic Church, New York: Alba House,
      1967.

Ott, Ludwig, Fundamentals of Catholic Dogma, St. Louis: B. Herder Book Company, 1957.

B. Secondary Sources

1. Books

Abernathy, G.L., and T.A. Langford, eds., Philosophy of Religion, New York: Macmillan, 1962.

Abt, L.E., and L. Bellak, eds., Projective Psychology, New York: Knopf, 1950.

Adler, Gerard, The Living Symbol, New York: Pantheon Books, 1961.

Aiken, Henry David, Intellectual Honesty and Religious Commitment, Philadelphia: Fortress Press,
        1969.

Alfaro, Jumenez Juan, Man Before God: Toward a Theology of Man, New York:
        Blakinston-McGraw, 1966.

Allport, Gordon W., Becoming, New Haven: Yale University Press, 1955.

Altizer, Thomas, Mircea Eliade and the Dialectic of the Sacred, Philadelphia: The Westminster Press,
        1963.

Aquinas, St. Thomas, Summa Theologiae, New York: McGraw-Hill, 1964.

Barbour, Ian, Myths, Models and Paradigms: A Comparative Study in Science and Religion, New
        York: Harper and Row, 1974.

Bennet, Edward A., What Jung Really Said, New York: Schocken Books, 1967.

Birmingham, William, and Joseph E. Cunneen, eds., Cross Currents of Psychiatry and Catholic
    Morality, New York: Pantheon Books, 1964.

Bodkin, Maud, Studies of Type-Images in Poetry, Religion and Philosophy, London: Oxford
    University Press, 1951.

Bouyer, Louis, Dictionary of Theology, New York: Desclee and Company, 1965.

Braceland, Francis J., Faith, Reason and Modern Psychiatry, New York: P.J. Kenedy & Sons, 1955.

Browning, Don, Generative Man, Philadelphia: Westminster, 1974.

Buber, Martin, Eclipse of God, New York: Harper and Brothers, 1952.

Burrell, David B., Exercises in Religious Understanding, South Bend: University of Notre Dame,
    1974.

Caruso, Igor A., Existential Psychology, New York: Herder and Herder, 1964.

Cattell, Raymond B., Psychology and the Religious Quest, London: Nelson and Sons, 1938.

Clifford, Paul Rowntree, Interpreting Human Experience, London: Collins, 1971.

Cobb, John, A Christian Natural Theology, Philadelphia: The Westminster Press, 1965.

Connell, Francis J., Outlines of Moral Theology, Milwaukee: Bruce Publishing Company, 1953.

Cousins, Ewert H., Hope and the Future of Man, Philadelphia: Fortress, 1972.

Cox, David, Jung and St. Paul, New York: Association Press, 1959.

_____. Modern Psychology: The Teaching of Carl Gustav Jung, New York: Barnes & Noble, 1969.

Cruchon, Georges, Dynamic Psychology, New York: Sheed and Ward, 1965.

Curatorium of the C.G. Jung Institute, eds., Conscience, Evanston: Northwestern University Press,
        1970.

Curran, Charles, Absolutes in Moral Theology, Washington, D.C.: Corpus Books, 1968.

Dallett, Kent M., Problems of Psychology, New York: Wiley, 1969.

Deese, James, Principles of Psychology, Boston: Allyn and Bacon, 1964.

Dewart, Leslie, Religion, Language and Truth, New York: Herder and Herder, 1970.

Donceel, Joseph J., Philosophical Anthropology, New York: Sheed and Ward, 1967.

_____. Philosophical Psychology, New York: Sheed and Ward, 1955.

Douglas, Mary, Natural Symbols: Explorations in Cosmology, New York: Pantheon Books, 1970.

Dry, Avis M., The Psychology of Jung: A Critical Interpretation, London: Methuen & Co., 1961.

Dudley, Guilford, The Recovery of Christian Myth, Philadelphia: Westminster Press, 1968.

Dulles, Avery, The Survival of Dogma, New York: Image, 1973.

Dupre, Louis, The Other Dimension: A Search for the Meaning of Religious Attitudes, New York:
	Doubleday, 1972.

Eliade, Mircea, Images and Symbols, New York: Sheed and Ward, 1961.

_____. The Forge and the Crucible, New York: Harper, 1962.

Ellenberger, Henri, The Discovery of the Unconscious, New York: Basic Books, 1970.

Evans, Richard I, Conversations with Carl Jung, Princeton: D. Van Nostrand Co., 1964.

Feaver, J. Clayton, and Wm. Horosz, Religion in Philosophical and Cultural Perspective, New York:
	D. Van Nostrand Co., 1967.

Fesquest, Henri, Catholicism: Religion of Tomorrow, New York: Holt, Rinehart and Winston, 1964.

Flew, Robert Newton, The Idea of Perfection in Christian Theology, London: Oxford University
	Press, 1934.

Fordham, Michael, The Objective Psyche, London: Routledge and Kegan Paul, 1958.

Franz, Marie-Louise von, C.G. Jung: His Myth in Our Time, New York: C.G. Jung Foundation and
	G.P. Putnam's Sons, 1975.

Frayn, R. Scott, Revelation and the Unconscious, London: The Epworth Press, 1940.

Fremantle, Anne, The Age of Belief, Boston: Houghton Mifflin, 1957.

Frey-Rohn, Liliane, From Freud to Jung: A Comparative Study of the Psychology of the
      Unconscious, New York: Engreen, 1974.

Frischknecht, Max, Die Religion in der Psychologie C.G. Jungs, Berne, 1945.

Gelpi, Albert J., The Tenth Muse, Cambridge: Harvard University Press, 1975.

Gemelli, Agnostino, Psychoanalysis Today, New York: P.J. Kenedy & Sons, 1955.

Gilkey, Langdon, Naming the Whirlwind: The Renewal of God-Language, New York:
      Bobbs-Merrill, 1969.

Gilson, Etienne, God and Philosophy, New Haven: Yale University Press, 1944.

Glover, Edward, Freud or Jung, New York: W.W. Norton & Co., 1950.

Godin, Andre, Child and Adult Before God, Chicago: Loyola University Press, 1965.

_____. The Pastor as Counselor, New York: Holt, Rinehart and Winston, 1965.

Goldbrunner, Josef, Cure of Mind and Cure of Soul, New York: Pantheon, 1958.

_____. <u>Holiness is Wholeness</u>, New York: Pantheon, 1955.

_____. <u>Individuation</u>, New York: Pantheon, 1956.

_____. <u>Sprechzimmer und Beichstuhl uber Religion und Psychologie</u>, Freiburg: Herder-Bucherei,
　　　　1967.

Haering, Bernard, <u>Morality Is For Persons</u>, New York: Farrar, Strauss and Giroun, 1971.

Hall, Calvin S., and Vernon J. Nordby, <u>A Primer of Jungian Psychology</u>, New York: New American
　　　　Library, 1973.

Hall, Calvin, and Gardner Lindzey, <u>Theories of Personality</u>, New York: John Wiley & Sons, Inc.,
　　　　1970.

Hanna, Charles Bartruff, <u>The Face of the Deep</u>, Philadelphia: The Westminster Press, 1968.

Harding, Mary Esther, <u>Journey Into Self</u>, New York: Longmans, Green, 1956.

_____. <u>Psychic Energy: Its Source and Its Transformation</u>, New York: Pantheon Books, 1963.

_____. <u>The Parental Image</u>, New York: Putnam, 1965.

Hartshorne, Charles, <u>Man's Vision of God</u>, Chicago: Willet, Clark and Company, 1941.

Henry, A.M., ed., <u>Man and His Happiness</u>, Vol. III, Chicago: Fides Publishers Association, 1956.

Hillman, James, <u>Insearch: Psychology and Religion</u>, New York: C. Scribner's, 1967.

_____. <u>Re-visioning Psychology</u>, New York: Harper & Row, 1975.

_____. <u>The Myth of Analysis: Three Essays in Archetypal Psychology</u>, Evanston: Northwestern
   University Press, 1972.

Hochheimer, Wolfgang, <u>The Psychotherapy of C.G. Jung</u>, New York: G.P. Putnam's Sons, 1969.

Holt, Edwin B., <u>The Freudian Wish</u>, New York: Holt, 1951.

Homans, Peter, ed., <u>The Dialogue Between Theology and Psychology</u>, Chicago: The University of
   Chicago Press, 1968.

Hostie, Raymond, <u>Religion and the Psychology of Jung</u>, New York: Sheed and Ward, 1957.

Hutchison, John A., <u>Language and Faith</u>, Philadelphia: The Westminster Press, 1963.

Jacobi, Jolande, <u>Complex, Archetype, Symbol in the Psychology of C.G. Jung</u>, New York: Pantheon
   Books, 1959.

_____. <u>The Way of Individuation</u>, New York: Harcourt, Brace & World, 1967.

Jaffe, Aniela, <u>From the Life and Work of C.G. Jung,</u> New York: Harper & Row, 1971.

Jaffe, Aniela, ed., <u>C.G. Jung: Word and Image</u>, Princeton: Princeton University Press, Bollinger
   Series XCVII:2, 1979.

James, William, <u>The Varieties of Religious Experience</u>, New York: Longmans, 1952.

Jansen, G.M.A., <u>An Existential Approach to Theology</u>, Milwaukee: The Bruce Publishing Company,
    1966.

Jones, Ernest, <u>The Life and Works of Sigmund Freud</u>, New York: Basic Books, 1957.

Kirk, G.S., <u>Myth: Its Meaning and Functions in Ancient and Other Cultures</u>, Berkeley: University of
    California Press, 1971.

Kirk, Kenneth Escott, <u>The Vision of God</u>, New York: Harper and Row, 1966.

Kohl, Herbert, <u>The Age of Complexity</u>, New York: New American Library, 1965.

Lamb, George Robert, ed., <u>Religion and the Psychology of Jung</u>, New York: Sheed and Ward, 1957.

London, Perry, <u>The Modes and Morals of Psychotherapy</u>, New York: Holt, Rinehart & Winston,
    1964.

Long, Edward Le Roy, <u>The Role of the Self in Conflicts and Struggle</u>, Philadelphia: Westminster
    Press, 1962.

Lonergan, Bernard, <u>Doctrinal Pluralism</u>, Milwaukee: Marquette University Press, 1971.

_____. <u>Insight: A Study of Human Understanding</u>, London: Longmans, Green & Company, 1957.

_____. Method in Theology, New York: Herder and Herder, 1972.

Mackey, James, Modern Theology of Tradition, New York: Herder and Herder, 1962.

Macquarrie, John, Principles of Christian Theology, New York: Charles Scribner's Sons, 1966.

_____. Thinking about God, New York: Harper & Row, 1975.

_____. Twentieth-century Religious Thought: The Frontiers of Philosophy and Theology, London: S.C.M. Press, 1971.

Meier, Carl Alfred, Ancient Incubation and Modern Psychotherapy, Evanston: Northwestern
        University Press, 1967.

Miles, T.R., Religious Experience, London: St. Martin's Press, 1972.

Milhaven, John Giles, Toward a New Catholic Morality, Garden City: Doubleday, 1970.

Moran, Gabriel, Catechesis of Revelation, New York: Herder and Herder, 1966.

Moreno, Antonio, Jung, Gods and Modern Man, South Bend: University of Notre Dame Press,
        1970.

Moroux, Jean, I Believe: The Personal Structure of Faith, New York: Sheed and Ward, 1959.

_____. The Christian Experience, New York: Sheed and Ward, 1954.

_____. The Meaning of Man, New York: Sheed and Ward, 1948.

Murchland, Bernard, The New Iconoclasm: Reflections for a Time of Transition, New York: Dell,
 1973.

Mygren, Anders, Meaning and Method: Prolegomena to a Scientific Philosophy of Religion and a
 Scientific Theology, Philadelphia: Fortress, 1972.

Oraison, Marc, Being Together, Garden City: Doubleday & Company, 1970.

_____. Illusion and Anxiety, New York: Macmillan, 1963.

_____. Love or Constraint?, Glen Rock, New Jersey: Paulist Press, 1961.

_____. The Wound of Mortality, Garden City: Doubleday, 1971.

Ornstein, Robert E., ed., The Nature of Human Consciousness, San Francisco: W.H. Freeman and
 Company, 1973.

Otto, Rudolf, The Idea of the Holy, London: Oxford University Press, 1943.

Padovano, Anthony T., The Estranged God, New York: Sheed and Ward, 1966.

Parente, Pietro, et. al., Dictionary of Dogmatic Theology, Milwaukee: Bruce Publishing Company,
 1951.

Pattison, E. Mansell, ed., Clinical Psychiatry and Religion, Boston: Little, Brown and Company,
 1969.

Philipson, Morris, <u>Outline of a Jungian Aesthetics</u>, Evanston: Northwestern University Press, 1963.

Progoff, Ira, <u>Jung's Psychology and its Social Meaning</u>, Garden City: Doubleday, 1973.

_____. <u>The Death and Rebirth of Psychology</u>, New York: McGraw-Hill Book Company, 1973.

Ramsey, Ian, <u>Religious Language: An Empirical Placing of Theological Phrases</u>, New York:
     Macmillan, 1967.

_____. <u>Words About God</u>, London: S.C.M. Press, 1971.

Rieff, Philip, <u>Freud: The Mind of the Moralist</u>, Garden City: Doubleday and Company, 1961.

_____. <u>The Triumph of the Therapeutic</u>, New York: Harper and Row, 1968.

Rohrbach, Elizabeth C., ed., <u>Jung's Contribution to our Time: The Collected Papers of Eleanor</u>
     <u>Bertine</u>, New York: G.P. Putnam's Sons, 1967.

Schaer, Hans, <u>Religion and the Cure of Souls in Jung's Psychology</u>, New York: Pantheon Books,
     1950.

Sheed, F.J., <u>God and the Human Condition</u>, New York: Sheed and Ward, 1966.

Smith, Robert D., <u>The Mark of Holiness</u>, Westminster, Maryland: The Newman Press, 1961.

Stern, Karl, <u>The Third Revolution: A Study of Psychiatry and Religion</u>, New York: Harcourt, Brace
     and Company, 1954.

Swanson, Guy L., Birth of the Gods, Ann Arbor: University of Michigan, 1960.

Toynbee, Philip, The Age of the Spirit: Religion as Experience, New York: Harper & Row, 1973.

Trethhowan, Illtyd, The Basis of Belief, New York: Hawthorn Books, 1961.

Trueblood, David E., Philosophy of Religion, New York: Harper, 1957.

Ulanov, Ann Belford, The Feminine in Jungian Psychology and in Christian Theology, Evanston:
    Northwestern University Press, 1971.

Van der Leeuw, G., Religion in Essence and Manifestation, London: Allen Unwin, 1938.

Van der Post, Laurens, Jung and the Story of Our Time, New York: Pantheon, 1975.

Vander Veldt, James J. and Robert P. Odenwald, Psychiatry and Catholicism, New York:
    McGraw-Hill Book Company, 1952.

Walgrave, Jan Hendrik, Unfolding Revelation, Philadelphia: Westminster, 1972.

Ward, Keith, The Concept of God, New York: St. Martin's Press, 1974.

Weigel, Gustave, Catholic Theology in Dialogue, New York: Harper, 1961.

White, Victor, God and the Unconscious, Chicago: Henry Regnery Company, 1953.

_____. God and Unknown, New York: Harper and Brothers, 1956.

_____. Soul and Psyche, London: Collins and Harvill Press, 1960.

Whitmont, Edward C., The Symbolic Quest, New York, Putnam, 1969.

Wilhelm, Richard, The Secret of the Golden Flower, London: Routledge, 1931.

Winski, Norman, Understanding Jung, Los Angeles: Sherbourne Press, 1971.

2. Articles in Collections

Allers, Rudolf, "Psychiatry and the Role of Personal Belief," Faith, Reason and Modern Psychiatry,
        1955.

Beirnaert, Louis, "The Mythic Dimension in Christian Sacramentalism" Cross Currents of Psychiatry
        and Catholic Morality, 1964.

Bockus, Frank M., "The Archetypal Self: Theological Values in Jung's Psychology," The Dialogue
        Between Theology and Psychology, 1968.

Buonaiuti, Ernesto, "The Mystic Vision," Eranos Jahrbuch, Volume VI, 1970.

Choisy, Maryse, "Psychoanalysis and Catholicism" Cross Currents of Psychiatry and Catholic
        Morality, 1964.

Frei, Gebhard, "On Analytic Psychology: The Method and Teaching of C.G. Jung," God and the
      Unconscious, 1953.

Henderson, Joseph L., "C.G. Jung: A Personal Evaluation," Contact with Jung, 1963.

Marechal, J., "Empirical Science and Religious Psychology," Studies in the Psychology of the
      Mystics, 1927.

Rahner, Karl, "Pluralism in Theology and the Oneness of the Church's Profession of Faith," The
      Development of Fundamental Theology, Concilium 46, New York: Paulist Press, 1969.

_____. "The Historicity of Theology," Theological Investigations, IX, New York: Herder and
      Herder, 1972.

Stinnette, C.R., "Reflections and Transformation," The Dialogue Between Theology and
      Psychology, Studies in Divinity No. 3, Chicago: The University of Chicago Press, 1968.

Wili, Walter, "Aristotle's Ethics and the Psychology of Jung," Eranos Jahrbuch, Volume XII, 1946.

Zilboorg, Gregory, "Some Denials and Assertions of Religious Faith," Faith, Reason and Modern
      Psychiatry, 1955.

Zumstein-Preiswerk, Stefanie, C.G. Jung's Medium Die Geschichte der Helly Preiswerk, Munich: Kindler, 1975.

3. Articles in Periodicals

Allers, R., "The Undiscovered Self," Critic, 16:43, July, 1958.

Arens, R., "C.G. Jung and Some Far Eastern Parallels," Cross Currents, 23:73-91, September 1973.

Beirnaert, L., "C.G. Jung est Mort," Etudes, 310:124, August 1961.

_____. "Does Sanctification Depend Upon Psychic Structure?" Cross Currents, No. 2, Winter 1951.

Borelli, J., "Dreams, Myths and Religious Symbolism" Thought, 50:56-66, March 1975.

Braybrooke, N., "C.J. Jung and Teilhard de Chardin," Month, 39: 96-104, February 1968.

Brunner, A., "Theologie oder Tiefenpsychologie?", Stimmen, 152: 401-415.

Clark, G., "The Truly Sapient Hominid: Jung and the Unconscious," Philosophy Today, 17:205-12, Fall 1973.

Crehan, J., "Answer to Job," Theological Studies, 16:414-23. September 1955.

Crowley, T., "Jung and Religion," Irish Theological Quarterly, 23:73-79, January 1956.

Douglas, William, "The Influence of Jung's Work: A Critical Comment," Journal of Religion and Health, 6, No. 3, 1962.

Dourley, J., "Carl Jung and Contemporary Theology," Ecumenist, 12:90-95, September-October 1974.

Elkisch, F., "Answer to Job," Tablet, 205:135, February 5, 1955.

_____. "Some Practical Points of Jung's Analytical Psychology," Blackfriars, 27:461-6, December
    1946.

Ferre, F., "Mapping the Logic of Models in Science and Theology," The Christian Scholar, 48, No.1,
    9-39, Spring 1963.

Gaffney, J., "Symbolism of the Mass in Jung's Psychology," R.U. Ottawa, 33:214-31,
    October-December 1963.

Gemelli, A., "La Psychologie Analytique de C.G. Jung," Vie Spirituelle Suppl., No. 36, 44-80,
    February 1956.

Godin, Andre, "Therapeutic and Pastoral Work," Life of the Spirit, October 1957.

Harms, Ernest, "Carl Gustav Jung-Defender of Freud and the Jews," The Psychiatric Quarterly, XX,
    No.2 , 199-230, April 1946.

Haynes, R., "Interpretation of Nature and the Psyche," Tablet, 207: 134, February 1956.

_____. "Carl Gustav Jung: Exploring Uncharted Territory," Tablet, 215:577-78, June 17, 1961.

_____. "Man and His Symbols," Tablet, 219:40, January 9, 1965.

Heisig, James W., "Jung and Theology: A Bibliographical Essay," Spring, 1973.

Heym, G., "Review of Jung's Collected Works, Volume 12," Tablet, 202:230, September 5, 1953.

Jung, C.G., "Letter to Upton Sinclair," New Republic, February 21, 1955.

Kehoe, R., "Antwort auf Hiob," Dominican Studies, 5:228-31, 1952.

Layard, D., "Memories, Dreams, Reflections," Blackfriars, 44:531, December 1963.

LeBlanc, A., "The Undiscovered Self," Catholic World, 187:468, September 1958.

Leonard, A., "La Psychologie religieuse de Jung," Supplement de la Vie Spirituelle, 1951.

McLeish, J., "Carl Jung, Psychology and Catholicism," Wiseman, 235:264-276, Fall 1961.

_____. "Carl Jung, Psychology and Catholicism," Wiseman, 235:313-18, Winter 1961.

Mailhiot, B., "Achievement of Jung," Tablet, 206-103, July 1955.

Meissner, W.W., "Origen and the Analytic Psychology of Symbolism: The Canticle of Canticles,"
      Downside, 79:201-16, Summer 1961.

Merlin, E., "Faith and Psyche: A Role for Jung in Theology," Catholic World, 209:172-5, July 1979.

Meyers, J., "Freud/Jung Letters," Commonweal, 101:41-3, October 11, 1974.

Moloney, R., "Interpretation of Nature and the Psyche," Month, 15:360, 1953.

_____. "Psychology and Religion: West and East," Month, 20:219-24, October 1958.

Moreno, A., "Jung's Ideas on Religion: West and East," Thomist, 31:282-320, July 1967.

Nordberg, R.B., "Jung: Passing of a Mystic," America, 105:699, September 9, 1961.

_____. "Mysterium Conjunctionis," Catholic Educational Review, 62:273, April 1964.

O'Meara, T., "Marian Theology and the Contemporary Problem of Myth," Marian Studies, 15:127-56, 1964.

Rudolph, A., "Jung and Zarathustra; an Analytic Interpretation," Philosophy Today, 18:312-18, Winter 1974.

Schwartz, C., "Jung and Freud," Integ., 7:20-4, July 1953.

Staerk, M., "Aurich: Jung's Library at Kusnacht," Critic, 22:70-71, December 1963-January 1964.

Stern, K., "Jung and the Christians," Commonweal, 58:229-31, June 5, 1953.

Thiry, A., "Jung et la Religion," Nouvelle Revue Theologue, 79: 248-276, March 1957.

Vandermeersch, P., "The Archetypes: A New Way to Holiness; The Work of C. Jung," Cistercian Studies, 10, No.1, 3-21, 1975.

Vann, G., "Collected Works of Jung, Volume 9," Catholic Educational Review, 58: 421, September 1960.

Veldt, J. van der, "Psychoanalysis Today," <u>American Ecclesiastical Review</u>, 134:139-42, February
     1956.

Watkin, E., "Answer to Job," <u>Dublin Review</u>, 229:337, Autumn 1955.

White, Victor, "Aion: Untersuchungen zur Symbolgeschichte," <u>Dominican Studies</u>, 5:240-3, 1952.

_____. "Collected Works of Jung, Volumes 1, 5," <u>Blackfriars</u> 38:442, October 1957.

_____. "Development of Personality," <u>Blackfriars</u>, 36:31, February 1955.

_____. "Four Challenges to Religion," <u>Blackfriars</u>, 33:203-7, May 1952.

_____. "Interpretation of Nature and the Pscyhe," <u>Blackfriars</u>, 37:83, February 1956.

_____. "Jung and the Supernatural," <u>Commonweal</u>, 55:561-2, March 14, 1952.

_____. "Jung on Job," <u>Blackfriars</u>, 36:52-60, March 1955.

_____. "Practice of Psychotherapy," <u>Blackfriars</u>, 36:52-60, March 1955.

_____. "Psychological Reflection," <u>Blackfriars</u>, 35:32, January 1954.

_____. "Psychology and Alchemy," <u>Blackfriars</u>, 35:125, March, 1954.

_____. "Psychotherapy and Ethics," <u>Blackfriars</u>, 26:287-300, August 1945.

_____. "Psychotherapy and Ethics: A Postscript," <u>Blackfriars</u>, 26:381-7, October 1945.

_____. "St. Thomas Aquinas and Jung's Psychology: A Review of Catholic Though and Modern
Psychology by W.P. Witcutt," <u>Blackfriars</u>, 25:209-19, June 1944.

_____. "Two Essays on Analytical Psychology," <u>Blackfriars</u>, 35:125, March 1954.

_____. "Two Theologians on Jung's Psychology," <u>Blackfriars, 36:382-88.</u>

_____. "Von den Wurzeln des Bewusstseins," <u>Blackfriars</u>, 35:125, March 1954.

4. Editorials and Usigned Periodical Articles

_____. "A Little Jung is a Dangerout Thing," <u>America</u> 92:612, March 12, 1955.

_____. "Aufsaetze zur Zeitgeschichte," <u>Blackfriars</u>, 28:138-40, March 1947.

_____. "Confession Good for the Soul," <u>Ave</u>, 81:4, February 26, 1955.

_____. "Doctor Jung: A Reply," <u>Commonweal</u>, 48:568-9.

_____. "Jung's Lectures at Yale, entitled Applied Psychology and Religion," <u>Commonweal</u>, 27:32,
November 5, 1937.

_____. "L'Energetique Psychique," <u>Etudes</u>, 294:139 August 1957.

243

_____. "Memories, Dreams Reflections," <u>Ave</u>, 97:24, June 8, 1963.

_____. "Modern Man in Search of a Soul," <u>Pax</u>, 23:270, February 1934.

_____. "Psychological Medicine and Catholic Thought," <u>The Month</u>, October 1956.

_____. "Psychology and Religion: West and East," <u>Catholic Educational Review</u>, 56:499, October
      1958.

_____. "Psychology and Religion: West and East," <u>Dominicana</u>, 43:333, Winter 1958.

_____. "Psychology and Religion," <u>Tablet</u>, 171:406, March 26, 1938.

_____. "Psychology and Religion," <u>Thought</u>, 14:335-6, June 1939.

_____. "Self," <u>Cross Currents</u>, 7:263-71, Summer 1957.

_____. "The Influence of Jung's Work: A Critical Comment," <u>Journal of Religion and Health</u> 6,
      No.3, 1962.

_____. "The Last Interview with Carl G. Jung," <u>Opera-Mundi</u>, Paris, 1961.

_____. "Theologians on Jung," <u>Cross Currents</u>, 7:283-87, Summer 1957.

_____. "The Psychogenesis of Mental Disease," <u>Catholic Educational Review</u>, 60:63, January
      1962.

_____. "The Structure and Dynamics of the Psyche," <u>Blackfriars</u>, 42:230, May 1961.

_____. "Zur Psychologie Westlicher und Ostlicher Religion," <u>Lumen</u>, 19:366, June 1964.

5. Miscellaneous Works

Aylward, J., "Archetypes and Natural Law," <u>Proceedings of the Second International Congress of</u>
    <u>Analytic Psychology</u>, Zurich, 1962.

Latshaw, Blair Summer, <u>The Function of Psychology in the Development of Christian Doctrine</u>,
    Drew thesis, 1921.

Rahner, Karl, et. al., eds., <u>Sacramentum Mundi</u>, New York: Herder and Herder, 1970.

Tillich, Paul, <u>Systematic Theology</u>, Chicago: The University of Chicago Press, 1967.

www.ingramcontent.com/pod-product-compliance
Lightning Source LLC
Chambersburg PA
CBHW070853290526
45795CB00001B/104